Well Read 2

SKILLS AND STRATEGIES FOR READING

Kate Dobiecka | Karen Wiederholt

SERIES CONSULTANTS

Mindy Pasternak | Elisaveta Wrangell

OXFORD
UNIVERSITY PRESS

OXFORD
UNIVERSITY PRESS

198 Madison Avenue
New York, NY 10016 USA

Great Clarendon Street, Oxford OX2 6DP UK

Oxford University Press is a department of the University of Oxford.
It furthers the University's objective of excellence in research, scholarship,
and education by publishing worldwide in

Oxford New York

Auckland Cape Town Dar es Salaam Hong Kong Karachi
Kuala Lumpur Madrid Melbourne Mexico City Nairobi
New Delhi Shanghai Taipei Toronto

With offices in

Argentina Austria Brazil Chile Czech Republic France Greece
Guatemala Hungary Italy Japan Poland Portugal Singapore
South Korea Switzerland Thailand Turkey Ukraine Vietnam

OXFORD and OXFORD ENGLISH are registered trademarks of
Oxford University Press

Editorial Director: Sally Yagan
Senior Acquisitions Editor: Pietro Alongi
Design Project Manager: Maj Hagsted
Senior Designer: Claudia Carlson
Production Layout Artist: Julie Armstrong
Image Editor: Robin Fadool
Production Manager: Shanta Persaud
Production Controller: Zai Jawat-Ali

ISBN: 978 0 19 476102 4

Printed in Hong Kong

10 9 8 7 6 5 4 3 2 1

ACKNOWLEDGMENTS

Cover art: Claudia Carlson

The publisher would like to thank the following for their permission
to reproduce copyright material: **pp. 7–8**, Russ Keen, "YEAR-ROUND
RV LIFE TAKES TONS OF LOVE", Aberdeen American News, July 3, 2005.
Used by permission of The Aberdeen (SD) American News. **p. 13**, From
WGBH Educational Foundation Copyright © 2006 WGBH/Boston. Used by
permission. **p. 20**, Sascha Matuszak, Panda travels from obscurity into global
spotlight, South China Morning Post, Dec 16, 2005. Used by permission of
South China Morning Post. **p. 25**, A CONVERSATION WITH: Ullas Karanth;
From a Childhood Ambition Comes a Quest to Save the Tiger, August 16,
2005, Claudia Dreifus (NYT); Science Desk, Late Edition - Final, Section F, Page
2, Column 2. Copyright The New York Times. Reprinted by permission. **p. 38**,
Cathy Cromell, Garden Guru: Howard Dill, National Gardening Association.
Reprinted by permission of the National Gardening Association/www.garden.
org. **pp. 41–42**, From LONG WALK TO FREEDOM by NELSON MANDELA.
Copyright © 1994, 1995 by Nelson Rolihlahla Mandela. By permission of
Little, Brown and Co. **p. 59**, "The Ironman" Ironman/World Triatholon
Corporation. Used by permission. **p. 74**, "Research Shows Benefits of Special
Olympics" © 2005 Special Olympics. Used by permission. **p. 81**, "Baby Emma
Isn't Talking Yet, But She's Saying Plenty" Used by permission of Robin
Rhodes-Crowell. **p. 87**, "Chinese Moss May Alleviate Alzheimer's Disease"
Article by Amy O'Connor from Vegetarian Times (July 1997). Copyright ©
Vegetarian Times. Reprinted with permission. **p. 105**, Elizabeth Weise,
"Echinacea: It works; oops, it works not," USA TODAY, Jul 28, 2005, D.9.
Reprinted by permission. **pp. 112–113**, This information was provided
by KidsHealth, one of the largest resources online for medically reviewed
health information written for parents, kids, and teens. For more articles like
this one, visit www.KidsHealth.org or www.TeensHealth.org. ©1995-2007.
The Nemours Foundation **p. 121**, Margaret Lowman, Life in the Treetops:
Adventures of a Woman in Field Biology, New Haven [Conn]: Yale University
Press, 1999. Used by permission of Yale University Press. **p. 126**, Iain Lundy,
Alexander Fleming: Discoverer of 'Miracle Drug' Penicillin, Scotsman.com,
Jan 27, 2005. **pp. 133–134**, Thomas H. Maugh, "They Found Their Nobel
Inside Their Stomachs," Los Angeles Times, October 4, 2005. Reprinted by
permission. **pp. 141–142**, "Penn State's Long-Held Secret: The President's
Salary" Copyright 2005, The Chronicle of Higher Education. Reprinted with
permission. **p. 146**, Betty Rollin, "Should You Tell?" AARP Magazine, July
& August 2005. **pp. 153–154**, "Deception Detection" SCIENCE NEWS by
CARRIE LOCK. Copyright 2004 by SCIENCE SERVICE, INC.. Reproduced with
permission of SCIENCE SERVICE, INC. in the format Textbook via Copyright
Clearance Center.

The authors and publisher would like to acknowledge the following
individuals for their invaluable input during the development of this series:
Macarena Aguilar, Cy-Fair College, TX; Sharon Allerson, East Los Angeles
College, CA; Susan Niemeyer, Los Angeles City College, CA; Elaine S. Paris,
Koc University, Istanbul, Turkey; Sylvia Cavazos Pena, University of Texas
at Brownsville, TX; Maggy Sami Saba, King Abdulaziz University, Jeddah,
Kingdom of Saudi Arabia; Stephanie Toland, North Side Learning Center, MN;
Jay Myoung Yu, Yonsei University at Wonju, Korea; Anthony Zak, Universitas
Sam Ratulangi, Manado, Indonesia.

Special thanks go to Barbara Rifkind for her support of the editorial team.

AUTHOR ACKNOWLEDGMENTS

Many thanks to Mindy Pasternak and Elisaveta Wrangell, the originators of
this series, for their inspiration and creativity. Heartfelt thanks also go to the
staff and students at Norwalk Community College for their input during the
development of this series. Finally, we are very grateful to Kathleen Smith,
Phebe Szatmari, and Pietro Alongi, and the Oxford University Press editorial
and design staff for all their hard work on this project.

Notes to the Teacher

Welcome to *Well Read*, a four-level series that teaches and reinforces crucial reading skills and vocabulary strategies step-by-step through a wide range of authentic texts that are meant to engage students' (and teachers') interest. *Well Read 2* is intended for students at the low-intermediate to intermediate level.

Each of the eight chapters in the book revolves around a central theme, but every text in a chapter approaches the theme from a different angle or level of formality. This provides multiple insights into the subject matter, while at the same time developing reading skills. Thus, students will be able to approach the theme with increasing fluency.

Well Read is designed so that all the activities, including reading, are broken up into smaller pieces, and each has specific goals so that all students, regardless of their individual level, can participate and succeed. The activities in the book support the approach that students do *not* have to understand every word of a text in order to understand its basic themes. Vocabulary strategies in each chapter allow students to feel more comfortable guessing the meanings of unfamiliar words or phrases based on their context.

Chapter Introduction

The opening page introduces the chapter's theme. Questions and photographs are designed to activate the students' prior knowledge, as well as stimulate some limited discussion before the previewing, reading, and post-reading activities.

Getting Started

This activity precedes each text or graphic component. It is designed to help students focus in on a more specific topic through reflection and discussion. It also introduces a small number of critical vocabulary words or phrases.

Active Previewing

Active Previewing asks students to read only brief and selected parts of the text, and then answer very simple questions that focus on this material. This activity encourages the notion that students do not have to understand each and every word of what they are reading. There is a strong emphasis on how to preview a wide range of genres, both academic and non-academic, including—but not limited to—newspaper articles, online texts, magazine articles, textbook articles, tables, charts, graphs, timelines, and graphics.

Reading and Recalling

The first reading activity asks students to read and recall. This approach is less daunting than being presented with an entire text, and it also allows the students to retain more. Recalling encourages students to be accountable for the material they read. While students build their short-term memories, they begin to process information more quickly and holistically. Perfect recall is never the goal.

Understanding the Text

After each text, students are presented with a two-part reading comprehension activity. The first part checks the students' comprehension of the most basic ideas expressed in the text, whereas the second part challenges the students to recall other key ideas and information.

Reading Skills

Among other essential skills, students are introduced to *Topic*, *Main Idea*, and *Supporting Details* in separate chapters, which allows them to practice and master each of these skills before progressing to the next. Earlier chapters present choices in a multiple choice fashion, whereas subsequent chapters require the students to write their own interpretations. The ability to think critically about the information that is presented in the text is a crucial part of being an active reader. Students are first taught to distinguish between facts and opinions, and later, inferences. In the final chapters of the textbook, students will be asked to find facts and opinions and to make inferences of their own.

Vocabulary Strategies

Students first learn that they can understand the general idea of a text without understanding every word; however, skipping words is not always an option, thus students are introduced to different strategies throughout the book that can help them determine the meanings of new vocabulary without using their dictionaries. All vocabulary activities use examples from the texts themselves, yet the vocabulary strategies taught can be applied universally to reading that students do outside class. Developing these strategies will allow students to become more autonomous readers.

Discussing the Issues

Every text ends with a series of questions that encourage students to express their opinions and ideas about the general subject discussed in the text. The questions are designed to be communicative in that they strike upon compelling issues raised in the text.

Putting It On Paper

Reading and writing are two skills that inherently go together. The writing activity complements the chapter texts, yet it is also designed to stand independently should the teacher decide not to read all of the chapter texts. Each *Putting It On Paper* activity offers two writing prompts; the teacher can allow students to choose between the prompts or can select one prompt for all students to use.

Taking It Online

Each *Taking It Online* activity guides the students through the steps necessary for conducting online research, based on the theme of the chapter. Teachers might opt to prescreen a select number of websites in advance, thus directing the students to more reliable and useful sites. *Taking It Online* finishes with a follow-up activity that enables the students to take their research one step further, in pairs or groups.

An Answer Key, a PowerPoint® Teaching Tool, and an ExamView Pro® Test Generator with customizable tests and quizzes are also available with each level of *Well Read* in the *Well Read Instructor's Pack*.

Contents

Welcome to *Well Read*

Well Read 2 is the second level in a four-level reading series that strategically develops students' reading skills, setting them up for success as critical thinkers.

There are eight chapters in *Well Read* and seven sections in each chapter: *Chapter Introduction, Text 1, Text 2, Text 3, Text 4, Putting It On Paper,* and *Taking It Online.*

Chapter Introduction

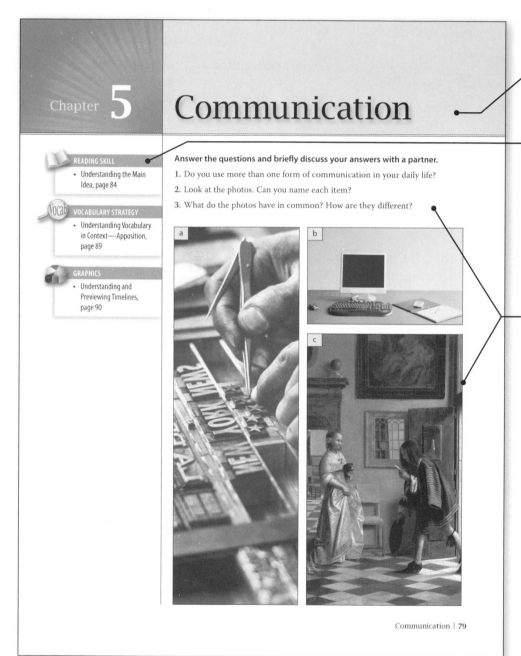

Chapter **5**

Communication

READING SKILL
- Understanding the Main Idea, page 84

VOCABULARY STRATEGY
- Understanding Vocabulary in Context—Apposition, page 89

GRAPHICS
- Understanding and Previewing Timelines, page 90

Answer the questions and briefly discuss your answers with a partner.

1. Do you use more than one form of communication in your daily life?

2. Look at the photos. Can you name each item?

3. What do the photos have in common? How are they different?

a

b

c

Communication | 79

• The opening page of each chapter introduces the **chapter's theme.**

• *READING SKILLS, VOCABULARY STRATEGIES,* and *GRAPHICS* boxes outline the main features of the chapter and focus students' attention on what they will learn. Page references allow for easy access to a particular area of focus.

• **Questions** and **photographs** activate the students' prior knowledge of the theme, as well as stimulate a brief discussion. Pre-reading discussion serves to activate or create some knowledge of the subject.

NOTE

Well Read is designed so that a chapter can be taught in its entirety or individual chapter components can be selected, depending on the amount of time available.

1 | Getting Started

A. Answer the questions and briefly discuss your answers with a partner.

1. Which types of transportation were used 150 years ago? Check (✔) all possibilities.

☐ a. airplane   ☐ e. horse-drawn wagon

☐ b. bicycle   ☐ f. hot-air balloon

☐ c. bus   ☐ g. ship

☐ d. car   ☐ h. train

2. How long might it take to travel from New York to San Francisco by the following means of transportation?

a. airplane _____   e. horse-drawn wagon _____

b. bicycle _____   f. hot-air balloon _____

c. bus _____   g. ship _____

d. car _____   h. train _____

Rethinking Travel | 11

Getting Started

Before each text, students **anticipate the more specific topic**—as opposed to the more generalized theme of the chapter—and a small number of **critical vocabulary words or phrases** is introduced.

---

2 | Active Previewing

Preview the magazine article below. Underline the title, the first sentence of each paragraph, and the last sentence of the text. Then answer the following questions with a partner.

1. What is the topic of the text?

2. Where is the language used?

3. Who is learning the language?

3 | Reading and Recalling

A. Read the text. Stop after each paragraph and tell a partner two things that you remember about it.

86 | Chapter 5

Active Previewing and Skimming

Students are taught how to **actively** preview a wide range of genres, both academic and non-academic, including newspaper articles, online texts, magazine articles, textbook articles, and graphics (see **Graphics** on page xii).

---

2 | Skimming

Skim the article in three minutes or less. Discuss your answers with a partner.

1. How old is Dr. J. Robin Warren? Dr. Barry J. Marshall?

----

2. In what year did the two researchers win the Nobel Prize in Medicine?

----

3. How much money did they receive?

----

4. What percentage of lower stomach ulcers are caused by Helicobacter pylori?

----

5. In what year did the research get its start?

----

3 | Active Previewing

Preview the academic text on the next page. Underline the title, the first sentence of each paragraph, and the last sentence of the text. Then answer the following questions with a partner.

1. What is the text about?

2. Which sentence that you underlined states the main point of the article?

132 | Chapter 7

The skill of **skimming** a text for general meaning is also introduced in later chapters.

Text 1, 2, and 4

The **texts** progress in length and level of difficulty in each chapter, and they are **authentic** in both presentation and content. Genres include: online texts, newspaper articles, magazine articles, and textbook articles, among others.

Caffeine

1. It's 11:00 P.M. and you've already had a full day of work or school. You're tired and you know you could use some sleep. But you still haven't finished everything you need to do or watched the movie that's due back tomorrow. So instead of going to bed, you reach for the remote—and the caffeine.

2. **What Is Caffeine?**
Caffeine is a drug that is naturally produced in the leaves and seeds of many plants. It's also produced artificially and added to certain foods. Caffeine is part of the same group of drugs sometimes used to treat asthma[1].

3. It is estimated that around the world people consume 120,000 tons[2] of caffeine annually[3]. Look at it another way. Every one of the 5 million people on the earth drinks one beverage—one cup—containing caffeine a day. Tea is the caffeinated beverage of choice.

4. Caffeine is defined as a drug because it stimulates[4] the central nervous system, the brain and spinal cord. Caffeine causes the heart to beat faster and makes a person feel wide awake. Most people who are sensitive to caffeine experience a temporary increase in energy. And they feel happier.

[1] **asthma:** an illness that causes difficulty in breathing
[2] **ton:** a unit of measuring weight equal to 2240 pounds
[3] **annually:** every year
[4] **stimulates:** makes a part of the body active

112 | Chapter 6

Online texts

Newspaper articles

Baby Emma Isn't Talking Yet, But She's Saying Plenty

BY ROBIN RHODES CROWELL

1. Emma and I are sitting on the bed as our cat jumps up. Emma looks at the cat, and then, without hesitation, takes both pointer fingers[1] and brushes them against her cheeks. It's her symbol for "cat."

2. Emma is learning baby signs. Baby signs are the same idea as American Sign Language (ASL)[2], but the parents and the baby determine the signs. The actual sign doesn't matter as long as everyone in the household understands it.

3. At 12 months old, Emma is too young to communicate with words. She is just starting to utter sounds that could be words such as "hat," "hot," and "hi." But she has a whole repertoire[3] of images and ideas that she communicates to us.

4. We started teaching Emma signs when she was seven months old. The motions are the same ones most infants use instinctively[4]. We started with "more" (pointer finger to palm), "bye" (waving), and "eat" (fingers to mouth).

5. We were pleased and rewarded when at nine months Emma started telling us she wanted more to eat. She moved on to more baby signs (nap, drink, book, bird, and others). Some we taught her and some she made up on her own!

6. Our experience with baby signs has helped us understand Emma's needs. One afternoon, after she and I had finished shopping at a bookstore, I put Emma into her car seat. As I handed her toys, each one was met with an upset look and an angry roar.

7. Emma then looked up at me with her big blue eyes and put her palms together and then opened them. I knew that she wanted a book to read. I gave it to her and she was happy. How incredible that, at 12 months, she was able to tell me exactly what she wanted.

8. For Emma, life without words is not a life without language.

[1] **pointer fingers:** the fingers next to the thumbs, often used to point at things
[2] **American Sign Language (ASL):** a communication system of hand signs used by people with hearing disabilities
[3] **repertoire:** the total number of things one is able to do
[4] **instinctively:** naturally, without thinking or learning

Communication | 81

Just Whistle

¹ People who live in La Gomera, a small island off the coast of Africa, are starting to whistle while they work again. But these are no ordinary songs.

² In fact, Silbo Gomero is not music at all, but a whistled language you can hear only on this hilly Spanish island. Researchers believe that Silbo Gomero first came to the island with settlers from Africa over 2,500 years ago. Residents are attempting to bring the language back to life before those who know it best, the shepherds¹, can no longer pass it on.

³ The whistled language is called Silbo from "silbar," the Spanish word for whistle. In the language, whistled sounds replace Spanish words. Sounds that are whistled higher or lower have different meanings. A Silbador, or whistler, can change the level of the whistle by using his fingers. The hilly terrain² of the region helps the sound travel. A Silbador can direct the sound even more by cupping the other hand like a megaphone³.

> The whistlers can communicate more than 4,000 words.

⁴ Whistlers do not simply pass along information about basic needs. They can carry on whole conversations. The whistlers can communicate more than 4,000 words. However, since some words sound similar, whistlers must sometimes guess the meaning.

⁵ In 2000, the local government required all school children in the island's fifteen schools to learn Silbo Gomero. Students between the ages of 7 and 14 practice the whistled language for half an hour a week. As a result, they can communicate with friends who live up to two miles away.

⁶ As many as 70 other whistled languages exist in areas with similar terrain: Greece, Turkey, China, Vietnam, and Mexico. But researchers have only studied 12. Each one is based on the language spoken in that area. Studying these languages is an important step in maintaining their existence. Modern communications systems, especially cell phones, now threaten them. The people of La Gomera hope that by teaching children their special language in school, they can continue to pass it on to future generations.

¹ **shepherds:** people who take care of sheep
² **terrain:** type of land, for example, a hilly area
³ **megaphone:** a piece of equipment that makes your voice louder

Magazine articles

---

4 | Reading and Recalling

A. Read the text. Stop after each paragraph and tell a partner two things that you remember about it.

Communication in the Internet Age: Facts and Trends

¹ **More Americans Online Than Ever**

According to a 2005 Pew survey¹, 68% of adults in the United States go online regularly, where they do a wide variety of things. Most use e-mail (91%). Many (84%) use search engines to find information. Two thirds buy products (67%). About half do job-related research. Others play online games (36%), listen to music (34%) or try to meet someone (27%).

² Men and women use the Internet in close to equal numbers, with men going online a bit more (69%) than women (67%). Not surprisingly, younger men and women log on much more often than older adults. For example, 84% of adults between the ages of 18 and 29 use the Internet. In contrast, only 26% of adults age 65 and older log on regularly.

³ The number of teens using the Internet is even higher (87%). More teens than adults use new technologies such as Instant Messaging (IM) and text messaging in order to connect with friends. Half of all teens surveyed use the Internet daily. In the last four years, teen use of the Internet has increased by 24%.

continued

¹ **survey:** a set of questions to get information about people's behaviors and opinions

04 | Chapter 5

Textbook articles

Understanding the Text

5 | Understanding the Text

A. Look at the photographs, and answer the question below without looking at the text.
Discuss your answer with a partner.

Which photograph best accompanies the text? Why?

_____

After each text, students are presented with a **two-part reading comprehension activity**. The first part checks the students' comprehension of the most basic ideas expressed in the text, whereas the second part challenges the students to recall other key ideas and information. Students are asked to complete as much as they can without looking back at the text.

Understanding the Topic, Main Idea, and Supporting Details

6 | Understanding the Topic

Answer the following question. Write *T* for *Topic*, *G* for *Too General*, and *S* for *Too Specific*. Discuss your answer with a partner.

1. What is the topic of the text?
   a. _____ babies and communication
   b. _____ words Emma knows
   c. _____ the success of baby sign language

2. Is your answer for the topic of the text the same as the one you determined after you previewed the text, or is your answer different? _____
   _____
   _____

Topic, Main Idea, and *Supporting Details* are introduced in separate chapters, allowing for **practice and mastery** before progressing to the next skill.

Practice Activities

3 | Scanning

Scan the pictograph for the answers to the questions. Discuss your answers with a partner.

1. Which category has the most endangered animals? _____
2. Which category has the fewest endangered animals? _____
3. About how many bird species are endangered? _____
4. About how many mammal species are endangered? _____
5. What is the total number of endangered animal species in the world? _____

4 | Discussing the Issues

Answer the questions and discuss your answers with a partner.

1. Should people support the preservation of all species, including insect species? Why or why not?
2. Which category of animal do you think gets the most public attention? Which gets the least? Why?
3. What do you think will happen to most of the species in this pictograph? Why?

A variety of activities allow students to practice the reading skills and vocabulary strategies, allowing for **recycling, review, and mastery.** (see *Reading Skills* and *Vocabulary Strategies* on page xi).

Discussing the Issues

Every text ends with a series of questions that encourage the students to **express their opinions and ideas** about the general subject discussed in the text.

Reading Skills

READING SKILL Understanding the Main Idea

The main idea of a text, section, or paragraph is the most important point the writer wants to express. For paragraphs, the main idea is usually the first sentence. The main idea is always expressed in a complete sentence.

To identify the main idea:

1. Look for the sentence that best expresses the most important idea of the text, section, or paragraph.

2. Reread the text to make sure that the main idea is not too general or too specific.

The topic of ¶1 on page 81 is *a sign that Emma is learning*.

Some possible choices for main idea are:

a. Emma and her mother are sitting on the bed.

b. Emma learns easily.

c. Emma knows a sign for "cat" and uses it to communicate.

Choice *a* is too specific to be a good main idea. It refers to a fact about Emma and her mother rather than an idea.

Choice *b* is too general to be a good main idea. It refers to a quality of Emma's and is not necessarily related to the topic.

Choice *c* is a good main idea. It tells us what the writer wants us to know about Emma. It relates to the topic because it mentions her use of the sign for "cat."

7 | Understanding the Main Idea

A. Text. Answer the following question. Write *MI* for *Main Idea*, *G* for *Too General*, and *S* for *Too Specific*. Discuss your answers with a partner.

1. What is the main idea of the text?

   a. _____ Babies cannot communicate in spoken language.

   b. _____ Even though babies cannot communicate in spoken language, they can be taught to communicate in baby sign language.

   c. _____ Only deaf babies should learn how to use sign language.

2. Is your answer for the main idea of the text the same as the one you determined after you previewed the text, or is your answer different? _____

_____

_____

84 | Chapter 5

- In each chapter, students are introduced to **new reading skills** and **vocabulary strategies**. They are always followed by a practice activity.

- The reading skills include ***Active Previewing, Skimming, Scanning,*** and ***Understanding the Topic, Main Idea,*** and ***Supporting Details,*** among others.

---

a. There are many whistled languages in the world.

b. Children on La Gomera are required to learn Silbo Gomero at school.

c. The people of La Gomera are trying to keep Silbo Gomero alive.

d. Studying whistled languages is important in keeping them alive.

 VOCABULARY STRATEGY Understanding Vocabulary in Context— Apposition

A word or phrase that means the same as a noun and is next to that noun in the sentence is said to be in **apposition** to the noun. Words and phrases in apposition are often set off by commas. Understanding and recognizing apposition helps a reader get more information from a text.

Read the following sentence.

Shepherds, *men who take care of sheep*, are the most expert whistlers.

In this example, *men who take care of sheep* means the same thing as *shepherds*. The phrase is in apposition to *shepherds*.

A word or phrase in apposition usually further describes a noun and has the same grammatical function in the sentence. In the example above, both *shepherd* and *men who take care of sheep* are subjects.

6 | Understanding Vocabulary in Context—Apposition

Write the words in apposition according to the text. Discuss your answers with a partner.

1. La Gomera (¶1) _____

2. those who know it best (¶2) _____

Communication | 89

Vocabulary Strategies

- Students are introduced to a variety of vocabulary strategies that can help them determine the meanings of new vocabulary **without using their dictionaries**.

- All vocabulary strategies present the vocabulary as it is used **in context**, yet the strategies themselves **can be applied universally** to reading that students do outside class.

Introduction to a Chapter | **xi**

Graphics

2 | Active Previewing

Preview the timeline below. Then answer these questions with a partner.

1. What is the subject of the timeline?
2. What are the two eras covered by the timeline?
3. Approximately how many years does the timeline cover?

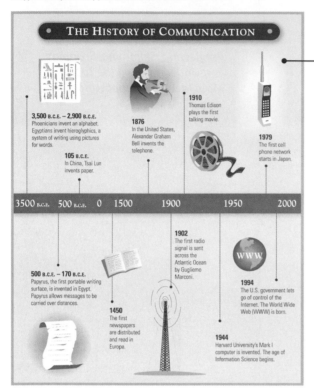

- Students are exposed to a **variety of graphics**. Text 3 of each chapter is always a **graphical representation on the chapter's theme.**

- The graphics include *Maps, Pictographs, Charts, Graphs,* and *Timelines*.

1. How much sleep do you get every night?
2. Do you ever worry that you aren't getting enough sleep? How much sleep do you feel would be the perfect amount for you?
3. Why do we need sleep?

2 | Active Previewing

Preview the bar graph on the next page and then answer the questions. Discuss your answers with a partner.

1. What is the title of the bar graph? How is the title related to the information in the graph?
2. What do you notice about the size of the animals in the graph, looking from left to right?
3. What do you notice about the number of hours of sleep, looking from left to right?

> **REMEMBER**
> Look for statistical information in bar graphs. Information is presented visually in vertical and horizontal directions. See page 45 for more on *understanding bar graphs.*

NOTE

Throughout *Well Read*, help is provided in the margin. *Remember* and *Online Tip* boxes give suggestions and page references to aid students as they work.

Putting It On Paper

A. Write a paragraph on one of these topics.

1. Should we look around the world for herbal cures for illnesses, even if they are not always found to be effective? Explain your ideas and give examples.

2. Can foods change your moods? Give specific examples to illustrate your opinion.

Steps for your paragraph

a. Write your opinion or main idea in the first sentence; this is your topic sentence.

b. Write three sentences with details—facts, data, examples, etc.—that prove your opinion or support the main idea.

c. Summarize your ideas in a final sentence.

B. Exchange paragraphs with a partner. Read your partner's paragraph and answer the questions in the checklist. Give feedback to your partner.

✔ CHECKLIST
1. Can you identify the main idea or your partner's opinion about the topic?
2. Are there three examples to support the topic? Number them on the paper.
3. Are you persuaded by your partner's examples or reasons? Explain below.
4. Is any of the information not related to the topic? If yes, please underline it on your partner's paper and then write it below.

C. Revis

Putting It On Paper

- In each chapter, students have the opportunity to write a **paragraph** based on the chapter's theme.

- The writing activity complements the chapter texts, yet it is also **designed to stand independently** if all of the chapter texts are not covered.

- Each *Putting It On Paper* activity offers **two writing prompts**.

Taking It Online | Researching Foods

A. With a partner, use the Internet to research foods that heal or cure.

1. Use Google (www.google.com) or another major search engine to find sites with the information you want. What words do you think you should type in the search box to begin your search? Write them here.

2. Preview the sites as you would a magazine article or an essay. Scan for information about three different food cures or remedies from three different countries.

B. Complete the table below with the information you find.

Type of food	Country of origin	Benefits	Problems
1.			
2.			
3.			

C. Following up. Tell your classmates about one of the food cures you discovered.

Taking It Online

- Every chapter culminates with a *Taking It Online* activity. This activity guides students through the steps necessary for **conducting online research**, based on the theme of the chapter.

- The online activity is **open** to the extent that students are encouraged to find their own sites, **but it is also focused** enough so that students will not be roaming through undirected data.

- *Taking It Online* finishes with a **follow-up activity** that enables students to **take their research one step further**, in pairs or groups.

Rethinking Travel

Answer the questions and briefly discuss your answers with a partner.

1. Do you like to travel?

2. Look at the photos and identify the types of transportation. Which have you used?

3. What is the farthest distance you have ever traveled? Where did you go and how did you get there?

Text 1 | Keep Running

1 | Getting Started

Answer the questions and briefly discuss your answers with a partner.

1. Is it possible for a person to run around the world?

2. What problems might you have if you ran a very long distance?

3. If you wanted to run around the world, where would you start? What countries would you run through?

4. How long do you think it would take a person to run ...

   a. ... across your city? _____

   b. ... across your country? _____

   c. ... across your continent? _____

   d. ... around the world? _____

 VOCABULARY STRATEGY Skipping Words

> When you read a text, you may come to words you do not know. A good strategy is to **skip these words**. You do not need to know the meaning of every word to understand the meaning of a paragraph or a text.
>
> However, if you find that a paragraph is unclear when you skip words, follow these steps:
>
> 1. Figure out the parts of speech of the words you skipped (noun, adjective, verb, adverb).
>
> 2. Think about what you understand.
>
> 3. Keep reading.
>
> Read the following sentence.
>
> She ran carrying her belongings in a 40-pound xxxxxxxx.
>
> What was she carrying that was 40 pounds? The text suggests that the skipped word is a noun: *She ran carrying her belongings in a 40-pound* "something." Think about what you understand: What do runners carry? It may not be necessary to know exactly what she was carrying, so we can skip the word and keep reading.

2 | Skipping Words

Read the sentences. Check (✔) the part of speech of the missing word.

1. For some time in the Alaskan wilderness, she pulled her belongings in a xxxx.

   ☐ a. verb   ☐ b. noun

2. She xxxxxxxxx between 10 and 25 miles each day.

   ☐ a. verb   ☐ b. noun

3. Rosie's adventures have included xxxxxxxxx, broken ribs, and pneumonia.

   ☐ a. verb   ☐ b. noun

4. She was trapped on an xxxxxxxxxx island in the Yukon river in Alaska.

   ☐ a. adjective   ☐ b. noun

READING SKILL Previewing Online Articles, Magazine Articles, and Academic Texts

Previewing will give you a general idea of what a text is about. To preview online articles, magazine articles, and academic texts:

1. Read the title and any subtitles.

2. Look at any pictures, graphs, or charts.

3. Read the first sentence of each paragraph.

4. Read the last sentence of the text.

---

3 | Active Previewing

Preview the magazine article on the next page. Underline the title, the first sentence of each paragraph, and the last sentence of the text as you preview. Then answer the questions with a partner.

What is the text about?

4 | Reading and Recalling

A. Read the text. Stop after each paragraph and tell a partner two things that you remember about it.

Around the World with Rosie

1   Rosie Swale-Pope is unlike any other 60 year-old grandmother in the world. Three years ago she left her house in Wales and started off on a solo[1] run around the world. With the exception of short flights between oceans, Rosie has run across Europe, Russia, and Siberia, and down through Alaska and Canada. She is currently crossing the United States and hopes to be home by next December.

2   When Rosie began her trip, she ran carrying her belongings in a 40-pound rucksack[2]. Later, a woman in Russia gave her a baby-jogger[3] to push. For some time in the Alaskan wilderness, she pulled her belongings in a sled. Now she pulls a cart she calls the "Silver Dream Machine". In it, she keeps her tent, cook stove, and other essentials. When full, her cart weighs nearly 300 lbs. Despite the weight, she averages between 10 and 25 miles each day.

3   Rosie's adventures have included incredible summertime heat and below-freezing winter weather, encounters with bears and wolves and robbers, frost-bite, broken ribs, and pneumonia. She even had to be rescued in a blizzard[4] where she was trapped on an uninhabited island in the Yukon river in Alaska. She has worn out over 36 pairs of shoes. Occasionally she has run out of food or money and is always grateful for the kindness of strangers she meets along the way.

4   When she has the opportunity, Rosie communicates with family and friends on a Website run by her son. People sometimes spot Rosie camping by the side of the road and talk with her or invite her home for supper. They often post on her Website how she has inspired them. In a letter to her fans, Rosie writes that "Running can take you to places that do not exist if you travel in any other way... You are treading[5] gently through someone else's land; Part of the life going on all around you—part of the people, places, sunrises, storms, terrors and joys..."

> "Running can take you to places that do not exist if you travel in any other way..."

---

[1] **solo:** alone

[2] **rucksack:** a backpack

[3] **baby jogger:** a special stroller to push a baby while running or jogging

[4] **blizzard:** a long, severe snowstorm

[5] **treading:** stepping or walking on

B. Read the text again without pausing. Tell your partner two new pieces of information that you remember.

C. Work as a class or in large groups. Say one thing you remember about the text.

5 | Understanding the Text

A. Complete as many statements as you can without looking at the text. Discuss your answers with a partner.

1. Rosie Swale-Pope is from

    a. Russia.   b. Wales.   c. Alaska.

2. Rosie Swale-Pope has already run across

    a. Canada.

    b. Australia.

    c. Peru.

3. Rosie's cart weighs up to

    a. 36 lbs.

    b. 40 lbs.

    c. 300 lbs.

4. Rosie enjoys

    a. meeting new people.

    b. running more than 25 miles per day.

    c. crossing rivers.

5. Most of the time, Rosie stays overnight in

    a. her tent.

    b. hotels.

    c. friend's houses.

B. Look at the map of the world. Without looking at the text, try to draw the route that Rosie is taking around the world.

6 | Discussing the Issues

Answer the questions and discuss your answers with a partner.

1. Why do you think Rosie is running around the world?

2. Do you think she will reach her goal? If so, how long will it take her?

3. Would you ever consider going on a journey around the world? If so, what form of transportation would you use?

Text 2 | Houses on Wheels

1 | Getting Started

A. Answer the questions and briefly discuss your answers with a partner.

1. Do you know how to drive? Do you enjoy driving?

2. What is the longest trip you have ever taken in a car?

3. What are the advantages and disadvantages of traveling by car rather than by other forms of transportation?

B. Read the statements. Check (✔) whether you agree or disagree. Briefly discuss your answers with a partner.

Statements	Agree	Disagree
1. Every adult should know how to drive a car.	☐	☐
2. It should be illegal to drive cars that use too much gas.	☐	☐
3. Cars are the most convenient form of transportation.	☐	☐
4. If there were better public transportation, fewer people would drive their own cars.	☐	☐

2 | Skipping Words

A. Read the following sentences. Cross out the words you do not understand. Then write their parts of speech on the blanks.

1. They bought a recreational vehicle and have been driving ever since.

_____

2. You have to want to be together. You have to be compatible.

_____

3. Never have the Webers regretted the extreme shift in lifestyle.

_____

4. The driver's seat is a comfortable living room chair that swivels around to face the windshield. _____

5. True, diesel is costly in the United States and the RV is not fuel-efficient.

_____

B. With a partner, discuss the parts of the sentences that you do understand.

3 | Active Previewing

Preview the online article below. Underline the title, the first sentence of each paragraph, and the last sentence of the text as you preview. Then answer the following questions with a partner.

1. What do you think the text is about?

2. The title of the text is "RV Nomads." What is an RV? What is a nomad?

4 | Reading and Recalling

A. Read the text. Stop after each paragraph and tell a partner two things that you remember about it.

RV Nomads

by Russ Keen

1   Nine years ago, Duane and Mary Jane Weber, both 56 at the time, said good-bye to their settled life in Osmond, Nebraska. They sold their newspaper and printing businesses, their cars, their home, and just about everything in it. They bought a recreational vehicle and have been driving ever since.

2   There are thousands of such people. Escapees RV Club reports 34,000 member families who are full-time RVers in the United States and Canada. Never have the Webers regretted the extreme shift[1] in lifestyle. It's not for everybody, though.

continued

---

[1] **shift:** change

continued

3   First, it takes a lot of love to make life on the road work. According to the Webers, you have to want to be together. You have to be compatible. Second, you have to enjoy the traveling lifestyle. Third, it's not for people who like to own a lot of stuff[2], because there just isn't room.

4   The driver's seat is a comfortable living room chair that swivels[3] around to face the windshield. Cruising[4] down the highway is like sitting in your living room and looking out a picture window at continually changing scenery, Duane said.

5   Scenery isn't the only pleasure of RVing, according to the Webers. The couple enjoys trying the various foods available around the continent. They prepare most of their own meals in the RV, however.

6   An RV can cost from 40,000 to 900,000 U.S. dollars, depending on the many features that are available. Once on the road, the main living expenses are food, clothing, and diesel fuel[5] to keep the RV moving, the Webers said.

7   True, diesel is costly in the United States and the RV is not fuel-efficient. Duane likes to tell people who ask about the gas mileage that it's "not great for a vehicle, but pretty good for a house."

---

[2] **stuff:** things
[3] **to swivel:** to turn
[4] **to cruise:** to drive easily
[5] **diesel fuel:** a type of gas

B. Read the text again without pausing. Tell your partner two new pieces of information that you remember.

C. Work as a class or in large groups. Say one thing you remember about the text.

5 | Understanding the Text

A. Complete as many statements as you can without looking at the text. Discuss your answers with a partner.

1. The Webers currently live

    a. in Osmond, Nebraska.   b. in Edmonton, Canada.   c. on the road.

2. A full-time RVer is

    a. a person who lives in   b. a form of transportation.   c. a type of fuel.
    a recreational vehicle.

3. The Webers

    a. wish that they had a regular house to live in.

    b. do not regret their decision to live in an RV.

    c. get great gas mileage in their RV.

B. Write *T* for *True* and *F* for *False* according to the text. Discuss your answers with a partner.

_____ **1.** Before they sold their house, the Webers owned a bookstore.

_____ **2.** About 10,000 families live in RVs full-time.

_____ **3.** Scenery and food are two of the things the Webers enjoy about RV life.

_____ **4.** RVs can cost between 40,000 and 900,000 U.S. dollars.

_____ **5.** RVs are very fuel-efficient.

6 | Discussing the Issues

Answer the questions and discuss your answers with a partner.

1. According to the Webers, what are the advantages and disadvantages of traveling full-time in an RV?

2. What do you think the average age of full-time RVers is? Do you think both younger and older families could enjoy this lifestyle?

3. Would you like to be a full-time RVer? Why or why not?

Text 3 | Moving Westward

1 | Getting Started

Answer the questions and briefly discuss your answers with a partner.

1. Have you ever moved to a new town? What are some of the difficulties of moving?

2. What form of transportation do people usually use to move from one house to another?

3. Before cars, trucks, and moving vans, how did people move from one place to another?

 GRAPHICS Understanding Maps

> **Maps** help people know where they are going. Maps can also help a reader better understand a text about history or geography. Many maps have a legend that shows distances and explains what the symbols mean.

2 | Active Previewing

Preview the map and its legend on the next page and then answer the questions. Discuss your answers with a partner.

1. What is the title of the map? What does it mean?

2. What area of the world does this map show?

3. Do you think this map shows modern roads or historic trails?

The Pioneer[1] Trails

Between 1843 and 1869, nearly 500,000 emigrants[2] known as pioneers moved to the West from the East Coast of the United States. They had heard stories of rich farmland and gold in the hills of California. The pioneers packed everything their families owned into covered wagons pulled by horses. Many families would travel together in groups called wagon trains. Below is a map of the trails that these wagon trains took to get across the country.

---

[1] **pioneer:** a person who goes to an undeveloped land to live and work there

[2] **emigrant:** a person who moves from one area or country to another

 READING SKILL Scanning Graphics

Scanning helps you find information quickly. You can scan for numbers, symbols, bolded items, names, key words, or brief answers to questions.

To scan a map:

1. Decide what you want to find: the name of a city, a road, a highway number, an airport, for instance.

2. Predict what signal will help you: capital letters, a color, a road, a symbol, a number.

3. Move your eyes quickly across the map to look for the item you want to find. For example, you might scan the map to find the line that shows the Oregon Trail.

3 | Scanning

Scan the map for the answers to the questions. Discuss your answers with a partner.

1. What are the names of the trails on the map? _____

_____

2. Which trail is the longest? About how long is it? _____

3. Which trail goes through Salt Lake City, Utah? _____

4. Which state is Santa Fe in? _____

5. Which trails would take a pioneer from Independence, Missouri, to Los Angeles, California?

_____

4 | Discussing the Issues

Answer the questions and discuss your answers with a partner.

1. Why do you think some of the trails are not straight lines between two cities?

2. How long do you think it took for a wagon train to get from Omaha, Nebraska, to Sacramento, California?

3. What dangers do you think the pioneers on a wagon train faced?

Text 4 | Laying the Rails

1 | Getting Started

A. Answer the questions and briefly discuss your answers with a partner.

1. Which types of transportation were used 150 years ago? Check (✔) all possibilities.

☐ a. airplane   ☐ e. horse-drawn wagon

☐ b. bicycle   ☐ f. hot-air balloon

☐ c. bus   ☐ g. ship

☐ d. car   ☐ h. train

2. How long might it take to travel from New York to San Francisco by the following means of transportation?

a. airplane _____   e. horse-drawn wagon _____

b. bicycle _____   f. hot-air balloon _____

c. bus _____   g. ship _____

d. car _____   h. train _____

B. Answer the questions and briefly discuss your answers with a partner.

1. Have you ever traveled by train? Do you enjoy it?

2. What are some of the advantages and disadvantages of train travel?

3. What materials are needed to build train tracks?

2 | Skipping Words

A. Read the following sentences. Cross out the words you do not understand. Then write their parts of speech on the blanks.

1. Many people believed that a railroad to the Pacific would be the future of the country and the answer to the problems of western migration.

   _____

2. Thousands of Civil War veterans also worked on the Union Pacific.

   _____

3. Union Pacific workers endured 12-hour shifts in the summer heat.

   _____

4. Avalanches and explosions killed more than a thousand workers.

   _____

5. The only towns along the route were the wealthy Mormon communities of the Salt Lake Valley in Utah.

   _____

B. With a partner, discuss the parts of the sentences that you do understand.

3 | Active Previewing

Preview the academic text on the next page. Underline the title, the first sentence of each paragraph, and the last sentence of the text as you preview. Then answer the following questions with a partner.

1. What is the text about?

2. What class do you think might assign this text?

4 | Reading and Recalling

A. Read the text. Stop after each paragraph and tell a partner two things that you remember about it.

The Iron Road

1 In the 1860s, the Civil War[1] divided America between the north and the south. But even before the Civil War, America was a divided country. Most people lived along the east coast. In the west, California was a large and rich area, but it was almost impossible to travel there. People in the east heard stories of gold and good, cheap farmland in the west, and they wanted to go. There were two ways to reach California: by ship or by covered wagon. It took months of dangerous sailing around Cape Horn to reach California by ship. Traveling 2,000 miles by wagon train across dangerous mountains and deserts often took almost a year. Many people believed that a railroad to the Pacific would be the future of the country and the answer to the problems of western migration[2].

2 In 1862, the American government decided on a route that went from Omaha, Nebraska, to Sacramento, California. Much of the route was along an old pioneer trail. They chose two companies to build the railroad. The Central Pacific would build from the west and the Union Pacific would build from the east.

3 The Central Pacific Railroad was started by a young engineer named Theodore Judah. The high Sierra Nevada Mountains in California always made a railroad across America seem impossible. Judah found a way to lay the tracks through the mountains.

4 The real heroes of the railroad were the 20,000 men who worked to build "the iron[3] road" with their bare hands. Most of the workers were immigrants. Almost 10,000 Chinese immigrants worked for the Central Pacific Railroad.

The Union Pacific workers were mostly from Ireland, Germany, the Netherlands, and the Czech Republic. Thousands of Civil War veterans also worked on the Union Pacific.

5 Life was hard for workers of both companies. Union Pacific workers endured 12-hour shifts in the summer heat. Sometimes, violent groups of people attacked the camps. The Central Pacific workers also had long shifts. They had the dangerous job of building the railroad across the Sierra Nevada Mountains. Avalanches[4] and explosions[5] killed more than a thousand workers.

6 As the railroad lines got closer, the two companies became competitive. The only towns along the route were the wealthy[6] communities of the Salt Lake Valley in Utah. The company that got to Salt Lake first could build a train station and get the profitable Salt Lake business. There was no finish line to this race, so the two railroad companies began to build right past each other across the high desert of Northern Utah. The government finally made the two companies agree on a meeting point. They agreed on Promontory, Utah, on the north rim of Salt Lake. It was here they finally met on May 10, 1869, six years after beginning the project.

---

[1] **Civil War:** the war between the northern states and southern states of the U.S., 1861–1865

[2] **migration:** the movement of animals or people from one area to another

[3] **iron:** a metal, Fe

[4] **avalanche:** snow, rocks, or mud that suddenly fall down a mountain

[5] **explosion:** noise and damage caused by bombs or dynamite

[6] **wealthy:** rich

B. Read the text again without pausing. Tell your partner two new pieces of information that you remember.

C. Work as a class or in large groups. Say one thing you remember about the text.

5 | Understanding the Text

A. Complete as many statements as you can without looking at the text. Discuss your answers with a partner.

1. "The Iron Road" is the name people gave to

   a. the railroad.   b. the pioneer trails.   c. a highway made of iron.

2. People thought it was impossible to build a railroad across the U.S. because of the

   a. hot temperatures.   b. avalanches.   c. high mountains.

3. The workers of the Central Pacific Railroad were mostly

   a. Irish immigrants.   b. Chinese immigrants.   c. Civil War veterans.

4. The workers of the Union Pacific Railroad were mostly

   a. from the Salt Lake Valley.

   b. Native Americans.

   c. European immigrants and Civil War veterans.

5. The two companies built the railroads from different sides and met in

   a. California.   b. Utah.   c. the Sierra Nevada Mountains.

B. Check (✔) the correct answers according to the information in the text. Discuss your answers with a partner.

Which company had problems with ...	Central Pacific	Union Pacific
1. ... avalanches?	☐	☐
2. ... high mountains?	☐	☐
3. ... violence?	☐	☐
4. ... explosions?	☐	☐
5. ... hot temperatures?	☐	☐

6 | Discussing the Issues

Answer the questions and discuss your answers with a partner.

1. Why did people want to travel west?

2. If you had lived in the 1800s before the railroad was built, would you have made the journey from the east coast to the west? Why or why not?

3. When were railroads built in some other countries? What transportation did people use before they were built?

Putting It On Paper

A. Write a paragraph on one of these topics.

1. What is your favorite form of transportation and why?

2. Do all communities need to have a public transportation system? Why or why not?

3. Should cities allow cars in the city center? Why or why not?

Steps for your paragraph

a. State your opinion about transportation in the first sentence; this is your topic sentence.

b. Write three sentences with details—facts and examples that support your opinion.

c. Summarize your ideas in a final sentence.

B. Exchange paragraphs with a partner. Read your partner's paragraph and answer the questions in the checklist. Give feedback to your partner.

✔ CHECKLIST
1. Does the first sentence state your partner's opinion? If so, summarize it below.
2. Are there three examples to support the topic? Number them on the paper.
3. Does your partner give good examples, reasons, or advice? Explain below.
4. Is any of the information not related to the topic? If so, please underline it on your partner's paper and then write it below.

_____

_____

_____

_____

_____

_____

_____

C. Revise your work based on your partner's feedback.

Taking It Online | Exploring a City

A. With a partner, use the Internet to research transportation.

1. Decide on a city that you would both like to visit. Make a list of three ways that you could travel to the city.

2. Use Google (www.google.com) or another major search engine to find sites with the information you want.

3. Preview the sites the same way you would preview a magazine article or an essay.

ONLINE TIP

Use key words to find information on a search engine:
Seoul Rome flight
New York Boston train
RV rental Canada

B. Complete the table with the information you find.

Three Ways to Travel from _____ to _____ (your location) (your destination)		
Form of transportation	**Cost**	**Travel time**
1.		
2.		
3.		

C. Following up. Tell your classmates the form of transportation that is best for your destination. Explain why.

Protecting Wildlife

Answer the questions and briefly discuss your answers with a partner.

1. An endangered animal is an animal that is at risk of dying out, or becoming extinct. Have you ever seen an endangered animal? Which animal? Where was it?

2. Identify the endangered animals below. Where do you think these animals live?

3. What are some reasons that an animal becomes endangered?

a

b

c

d

Text 1 | A Famous Endangered Animal

1 | Getting Started

A. Look at the photo and then answer the questions. Briefly discuss your answers with a partner.

A bamboo forest in China

1. Have you ever seen a giant panda?

2. Where do giant pandas live?

3. How many giant pandas do you think live in the wild, outside of zoos?

4. What do you think giant pandas eat?

B. Check (✔) the reasons you think giant pandas are endangered. Briefly discuss your answers with a partner.

☐ 1. disease

☐ 2. difficulty reproducing

☐ 3. forest fires

☐ 4. humans take over the land

☐ 5. humans kill them

☐ 6. other animals kill them

☐ 7. loss of food source

☐ 8. humans take them as pets

2 | Skipping Words

Read the sentences. Check (✔) the part of speech of the missing word.

1. The panda is also an international xxxxxxx of wildlife preservation.

   ☐ a. noun   ☐ b. verb

2. The panda's diet consists mostly of xxxxxxx.

   ☐ a. adjective   ☐ b. noun

3. Only about 1,000 pandas still xxxxxxxx in the wild.

   ☐ a. noun   ☐ b. verb

4. Unfortunately, pandas brought to zoos did not xxxxxxxxx and failed to breed.

   ☐ a. adjective   ☐ b. verb

5. Scientists try to make sure that all is well when the animals are xxxxxxxx back into the wild.

   ☐ a. noun   ☐ b. verb

READING SKILL Previewing Newspaper Articles

Newspaper articles usually arrange information from the most important to the least important.

To preview a newspaper article:

1. Read the title.

2. Look at any photographs, and read the captions.

3. Read the first two to four paragraphs. These paragraphs usually answer the questions *Who? What? When?* and *Where?* The rest of the article gives the details.

---

3 | Active Previewing

Preview the newspaper article on the next page by reading the first two paragraphs. Then discuss your answers to these questions with a partner.

1. What kind of animal is the article about?

2. Where is this animal from?

3. What does the Center try to do?

4. What do you think this text is about?

4 | Reading and Recalling

A. Read the text. Stop after each paragraph and tell a partner two things that you remember about it.

China's Giant Pandas

BY SASCHA MATUSZAK

1 China's giant panda is one of the world's most endangered species. An endangered species is a type of plant or animal with such a low population[1] that it may die out, or become extinct. The giant panda is also perhaps the best loved of all animals. People around the world think the panda is very cute, and toy pandas are always popular with children. The panda is also an international symbol of wildlife preservation[2].

2 Only about 1,000 pandas still exist in the wild. The panda population is very low because of the loss of the animal's natural habitat, a place where a plant or animal normally lives. Humans now use much of the land that the pandas once lived on. The panda's diet consists mostly of bamboo shoots, but the bamboo forests are also disappearing.

3 The giant panda has always been part of the culture of Chinese people. People in the west, however, first saw the giant panda in 1869. European biologists were puzzled by its appearance. They debated whether to categorize[3] the animal as a raccoon or bear.

4 In 1936, an American named Ruth Harkness made the long and difficult journey to China and Tibet to capture a panda. She returned to America with a baby panda named Su Lin. Zoos around the world wanted to own the animal. Unfortunately, Su Lin and other pandas brought to zoos did not thrive and failed to breed[4].

5 Serious research on pandas did not begin until the 1980s. The Wolong Giant Panda Reserve Center is in the Sichuan province of China. Scientists there research ways to save the panda. They are trying to

breed giant pandas to increase the population. They also take care of sick, injured, and lost pandas. The Center tries to make sure that all is well when the animals are released back into the wild.

6 Recently, the first captive-born[5] giant panda was released into the wild. The four-year-old panda named Xiang Xiang is doing very well so far. He was trained at the Wolong center to survive on his own. People around the world hope that scientists can release even more pandas back into the wild.

---

[1] **population:** the number of people or animals in an area

[2] **wildlife preservation:** the protection of wild animals in natural surroundings

[3] **categorize:** to put in a category or group

[4] **failed to breed:** did not get pregnant and reproduce

[5] **captive-born:** born in captivity, such as in a zoo

B. Read the text again without pausing. Tell your partner two new pieces of information that you remember.

C. Work as a class or in large groups. Say one thing you remember about the text.

5 | Understanding the Text

A. Look at the photographs, and answer the question below without looking at the text. Discuss your answer with a partner.

Which photograph best accompanies the text? Why?

_____

_____

B. Answer as many questions as you can without looking at the text. Discuss your answers with a partner.

1. Why are pandas in danger of extinction?

   a. because of the loss of natural habitat

   b. because of disease

   c. because of the Wolong Panda Reserve

2. What happened to pandas brought to zoos in the 1930s and later?

   a. They died immediately.

   b. They survived and thrived.

   c. They didn't reproduce and eventually died.

3. When did panda research and conservation begin?

   a. 1869

   b. 1936

   c. 1980s

4. What does the Wolong Giant Panda Reserve Center focus on?

   a. breeding, training, and caring for pandas to be released into the wild

   b. planting bamboo to increase panda habitats

   c. capturing pandas from the wild to keep in the center

5. What is the name of the first captive-born giant panda released into the wild?

  a. Su Lin

  b. Xiang Xiang

  c. Sascha

 VOCABULARY STRATEGY Understanding Vocabulary in Context—
Definitions

One strategy for understanding unfamiliar words is to look for a **definition** in the text. Sometimes, an important word or phrase is defined in the sentence that immediately follows it.

Read the following sentences.

China's giant panda is an *endangered species*. An *endangered species* is a type of plant or animal with such a low population that it might become extinct.

Note: In textbooks, the definitions of important words are sometimes found in the margin or in footnotes at the bottom of the page. For example, in the text "China's Giant Pandas," the word *population* is defined as "the number of people or animals in an area" at the bottom of the page.

6 | Understanding Vocabulary in Context—Definitions

A. Read the following sentences from *Text 1*. Check (✔) the part of speech for each underlined word. Then write its meaning on the line. Look for definitions in the text.

1. China's giant panda is one of the world's most endangered <u>species</u>.

  ☐ a. noun ☐ b. verb ☐ c. adjective

_____

2. The Panda population is very low because of the loss of the animal's natural <u>habitat</u>.

  ☐ a. noun ☐ b. verb ☐ c. adjective

_____

3. The panda's <u>diet</u> consists mostly of bamboo shoots, but the bamboo forests are also disappearing.

  ☐ a. noun ☐ b. verb ☐ c. adjective

_____

4. People around the world hope that scientists can <u>release</u> even more pandas back into the wild.

  ☐ a. noun ☐ b. verb ☐ c. adjective

_____

B. With a partner, try to define the following words. Then use the footnotes from the text to check your answers.

1. captive-born _____

2. categorize _____

3. failed to breed _____

4. wildlife preservation _____

7 | Discussing the Issues

Answer the questions and discuss your answers with a partner.

1. Why are giant pandas a good symbol of international wildlife preservation?

2. Do you think that the panda population will increase, decrease, or stay the same in the next 50 years? Why?

3. What else could people do to help increase the giant panda population?

Text 2 | Studying Tigers

1 | Getting Started

A. Look at the photo and then answer the questions. Briefly discuss your answers with a partner.

A forest in India

1. Have you ever seen a tiger?

2. What do tigers eat?

3. What is the natural habitat of the tiger?

B. Check (✔) the reasons that you think tigers are endangered. Briefly discuss your answers with a partner.

☐ 1. disease

☐ 2. difficulty reproducing

☐ 3. forest fires

☐ 4. humans take over the land

☐ 5. humans kill them

☐ 6. other animals kill them

☐ 7. loss of food source

☐ 8. humans take them as pets

2 | Skipping Words

A. Read the following sentences. Cross out the words you do not understand. Then write their parts of speech on the blanks.

1. When Ullas Karanth was a teenager in India, he read books by naturalists who were researching the tigers of Asia.

_____

2. The government says that there are more than 3,000 tigers. But preservation groups say the number is more like 1,000.

_____

3. But the biggest threat to tiger survival is habitat destruction and the uncontrolled hunting of the animals that tigers eat, like deer.

_____

4. Right now, about 5 percent of the country is designated as protected.

_____

5. All these factors make me hopeful that the tiger can be saved.

_____

B. Discuss the words you crossed out with a partner.

3 | Active Previewing

Preview the magazine interview on the next page. Underline the title, the first paragraph, the questions, and the last sentence of the text as you preview. Then answer the questions with a partner.

1. What is the text about?

2. Does Dr. Karanth think the tiger can be saved?

4 | Reading and Recalling

A. Read the text. Stop after each answer and tell a partner two things that you remember about it.

Saving the Tiger

BY CLAUDIA DREIFUS

1 When Ullas Karanth was a teenager in India, he read books by naturalists who were researching the tigers of Asia. "Someday, I'll study tigers, too," he told himself. Today Dr. Karanth is a leading tiger researcher and the director of the Wildlife Conservation Society's India Program.

2 Dr. Karanth was in New York to attend a conference[1] on the future of tigers in the wild. During a break, he spoke of his favorite feline[2].

3 **Q: Do we know how many wild tigers are still in India?**

We don't know. The government says that there are more than 3,000. But preservation groups say the number is more like 1,000.

4 At the Wildlife Conservation Society, we can only say that there are about 115,000 square miles of forest still left in the country where tigers can live.

5 **Q: Why are tigers disappearing?**

Poaching is part of it. Poaching is the illegal hunting of animals. The parts of a single dead tiger are worth something like $5,000. But the biggest threat to tiger survival is habitat destruction and the uncontrolled hunting of the animals that tigers eat, like deer. We have plenty of forest areas where there should be tigers, but their numbers are low there because deer have been hunted out by local people. So if you want to protect tigers, you actually also need to protect the deer.

6 **Q: How can we protect wildlife?**

To protect wildlife, you have to set aside some areas where human activities are reduced[3] or eliminated[4]. Right now, about five percent of India is designated as protected. But I estimate[5] that humans are active on most of that "protected" land. This needs to stop.

7 **Q: Do you think the Indian tiger can be saved?**

Certainly, if we try. India actually has more wild tigers than our neighboring countries. We won't need to reintroduce them. In addition, tigers reproduce easily; they are not like pandas.

8 Also, I believe that Indian culture can help encourage[6] conservation. In the Hindu religion, there is the belief that humans are a part of nature. I've talked with farmers whose crops have been destroyed by elephants, and they really hate them. But when I asked, "Don't elephants and tigers have the right to exist?" they always said yes. All these factors make me hopeful that the tiger can be saved.

> To protect wildlife, you have to set aside some areas where human activities are reduced or eliminated.

---

[1] **conference:** professional meeting, often at a big hotel

[2] **feline:** cat

[3] **reduced:** made smaller

[4] **eliminated:** stopped, removed

[5] **estimate:** guess

[6] **encourage:** help someone want to do something

B. Read the text again without pausing. Tell your partner two new pieces of information that you remember.

C. Work as a class or in large groups. Say one thing you remember about the text.

5 | Understanding the Text

Answer as many questions as you can without looking at the text. Then discuss your answers with a partner.

1. How many tigers are still in India?

    a. 1,000

    b. 3,000

    c. We're not sure.

2. Why are tigers disappearing?

    a. habitat loss from fire and avalanche

    b. poaching of tigers, hunting of deer, and habitat destruction

    c. difficulty breeding and disease

3. How can we protect wildlife?

    a. reintroduce tigers into Indian wilderness

    b. increase breeding programs

    c. reduce or eliminate human activity on protected land

4. Can the tiger be saved?

    a. Yes, because tigers reproduce easily and Indian culture respects animals.

    b. Yes, because there are still plenty of deer and other animals for tigers to eat.

    c. No, because the tiger habitat has been destroyed by elephants and farmers.

6 | Understanding Vocabulary in Context—Definitions

A. Define *poaching* according to the text.

Poaching is part of the problem. *Poaching* is _____.

B. With a partner, try to define the following words according to the text.

1. conference _____

2. eliminated _____

3. encourage _____

4. estimate _____

5. feline _____

6. reduced _____

7 | Discussing the Issues

Answer the questions and discuss your answers with a partner.

1. Who do you think estimates the tiger population more correctly: the government or the preservation groups? Why?

2. Why do you think people poach tigers? What are the parts used for?

3. Dr. Karanth believes that Indian culture can help encourage animal conservation. Do you know of other cultures that encourage animal conservation? If so, what do they do?

Text 3 | Animals in Danger

1 | Getting Started

A. With a partner, add more animals to the following groups.

1. insects _ant,_ _____

2. birds _chicken,_ _____

3. reptiles _snake,_ _____

4. mammals _dog,_ _____

5. fish _tuna,_ _____

B. Answer the questions and briefly discuss your answers with a partner.

1. Which of these animal groups do you think has the most species in it?

2. Which animal group do you think has the most endangered species in it?

3. Are there other animal groups besides those in part *A*?

 GRAPHICS Understanding and Previewing Pictographs

A **pictograph** is a graph that uses pictures to show information. To **preview** a pictograph, read the title, the rows, and the key. The key explains what the symbols mean.

2 | Active Previewing

**Preview the pictograph on the next page and then answer the questions. Discuss your answers with
a partner.**

1. What is the title of the pictograph?

2. What are the categories of animals?

3. How much does one 🐾 represent?

ENDANGERED SPECIES OF THE WORLD

🐾	MAMMALS[1]	🐾 🐾 🐾 🐾 🐾 🐾 🐾 🐾 🐾 🐾 🐾
🐦	BIRDS	🐾 🐾 🐾 🐾 🐾 🐾 🐾 🐾 🐾 🐾 🐾 🐾 (
🦎	REPTILES[2]	🐾 🐾 🐾 (
🐸	AMPHIBIANS[3]	🐾 🐾 🐾 🐾 🐾 🐾 🐾 🐾 🐾 🐾 🐾 🐾 🐾 🐾 🐾 🐾 🐾 🐾 🐾 (
🐟	FISH	🐾 🐾 🐾 🐾 🐾 🐾 🐾 🐾 🐾 🐾 🐾 (
🦋	INSECTS	🐾 🐾 🐾 🐾 🐾 🐾 (
🐌	OTHER INVERTEBRATES[4]	🐾 🐾 🐾 🐾 🐾 🐾 🐾 🐾 🐾 🐾 🐾 🐾 🐾 🐾 🐾 🐾 (

🐾 represents 100 different endangered species

---

[1] **mammal:** a warm-blooded animal that has a backbone and feeds milk to its babies

[2] **reptile:** a cold-blooded animal that has a backbone, lives on land, and usually reproduces by laying eggs

[3] **amphibian:** an animal that lives on both water and land

[4] **invertebrate:** an animal that has no backbone

READING SKILL Scanning Pictographs

Scanning is looking for information quickly. You often scan a pictograph to find out "How many"?

To scan a pictograph:

1. Find the key to learn what one symbol represents.

2. Move your eyes quickly down the column to find the word you are looking for.

3. Count the number of symbols in that row and multiply by the number that one symbol represents.

Read the following question:

How many insects are considered endangered species?

Refer to the pictograph. First look at the key to find the 🐾. Each symbol represents 100 different endangered species. Then, scan the column to find *INSECTS*. Next, count the number of 🐾s: about 6½, or 650 animal species. The answer is *650*. You do not need to read the other rows.

3 | Scanning

Scan the pictograph for the answers to the questions. Discuss your answers with a partner.

1. Which category has the most endangered animals? _____

2. Which category has the fewest endangered animals? _____

3. About how many bird species are endangered? _____

4. About how many mammal species are endangered? _____

5. What is the total number of endangered animal species in the world? _____

4 | Discussing the Issues

Answer the questions and discuss your answers with a partner.

1. Should people support the preservation of all species, including insect species? Why or why not?

2. Which category of animal do you think gets the most public attention? Which gets the least? Why?

3. What do you think will happen to most of the species in this pictograph? Why?

Text 4 | Discovered Again

1 | Getting Started

Use the words in the box to label the photos. Then answer the questions below and discuss your answers with a partner.

| coelacanth | mammoth | servaline genet | dodo | ivory-billed woodpecker |

a _____ b _____ c _____ d _____ e _____

1. Which of these animals do you think are extinct?

2. What do you think caused their extinction?

3. Do you think it is possible for an animal to return from extinction? If so, how?

2 | Skipping Words

A. Read the following sentences. Cross out the words you do not understand. Then write their parts of speech on the blanks.

1. According to the World Conservation Union, modern humans have caused a lot of damage to the earth's ecosystem.

   _____

2. Amazingly, in 1951, a small colony of birds was found off the islands of Bermuda.

   _____

3. The coelacanth is a strange, ancient fish.

   _____

B. Discuss with a partner what you think the crossed-out words mean.

3 | Active Previewing

Preview the academic text below. Underline the title, the first sentence of each paragraph, and the last sentence of the text as you preview. Then answer the following questions with a partner.

1. What is the text about?
2. What is one animal that has "returned from extinction"?
3. In what class would you read a text like this?

4 | Reading and Recalling

A. Read the text. Stop after each paragraph and tell a partner two things that you remember about it.

Returning from Extinction

1 According to the World Conservation Union, modern humans have caused a lot of damage to the earth's ecosystems[1]. In the past 500 years, humans have caused the extinction of 844 plant and animal species. But some animals that we thought were extinct have actually been rediscovered, or found again. This happens rarely but gives us cause for hope.

2 For 60 years, scientists thought the ivory-billed woodpecker was extinct. But in 2005, researchers in Arkansas found one of these large birds. Scientists and Arkansas citizens are now working to preserve the remaining habitat of this highly endangered species.

3 Recently, naturalists in Tanzania found another animal they thought had been extinct. The Lowe's servaline genet was last seen alive in 1932. For 60 years, naturalists had found only a single animal skin. In 2002, scientists were in East Africa studying carnivores, animals that only eat meat. They set

continued

---

[1] **ecosystem:** the community of living things in the environment

continued

up a camera trap in a remote[2] area. A camera trap is a camera left in the wilderness[3] to photograph an animal. When an animal walks past a camera trap, the camera takes a picture. When scientists saw the photographs, they realized that they had found a Lowe's servaline genet.

4   From time to time, scientists rediscover extinct animals after hundreds of years. A bird called the cahow was said to be extinct since the 1600s. The cahow was easy to catch. European colonists[4] living in Bermuda in the 1600s would eat them. Scientists believed that the colonists had hunted them to extinction. Amazingly, in 1951, a small colony of birds was found off the islands of Bermuda. The cahow had been hiding there for more than 300 years.

5   Another amazing rediscovery is the coelacanth. The coelacanth is a strange-looking ancient fish. Scientists had only seen the fish as a fossil: a collection of bones preserved in rock. They knew that the fish had lived around the time of the dinosaurs. Like the dinosaurs, it surely was extinct for the past 65 million years. In 1938, a naturalist named Marjorie Courtenay-Latimor found the strange fish in a fisherman's net in South Africa. In 1998, another colony of coelacanth was found in the ocean around Indonesia.

6   These animals show us that there is much that we do not know about our natural world. With the second chance that rediscoveries and recoveries like these have given us, perhaps we can take the opportunity to do a better job at preventing extinction.

---

[2] **remote:** a distant place

[3] **wilderness:** land in its natural state without human activity

[4] **colonists:** people governed by one country who move into a new area

B. Read the text again without pausing. Tell your partner two new pieces of information that you remember.

C. Work as a class or in large groups. Say one thing you remember about the text.

5 | Understanding the Text

A. Complete as many statements as you can without looking at the text. Discuss your answers with a partner.

1. Humans have caused the extinction of

   a. 60 species.   b. 500 species.   c. 844 species.

2. The ivory-billed woodpecker is a type of

   a. reptile.   b. mammal.   c. bird.

3. The Lowe's servaline genet was rediscovered when researchers

   a. accidently killed a genet in a trap.

   b. caught a genet and brought it to a zoo for further study.

   c. set up a camera to take photographs of wildlife.

4. The cahow became extinct in Bermuda because of

   a. people hunting the bird for food.

   b. poaching.

   c. habitat loss.

5. Before its rediscovery, people only knew about the coelacanth from

   a. photographs.

   b. skins.

   c. fossils.

B. Complete as much of the chart as you can without looking at the text. Discuss your answers with a partner.

Animal	Where was the animal found?	How long was it considered extinct?	When was it rediscovered?
1. Ivory-billed woodpecker			
2. Lowe's servaline genet			
3. Cahow			
4. Coelacanth			

6 | Understanding Vocabulary in Context—Definitions

A. Define *camera trap* according to the text.

They set up a *camera trap* in a remote area. A *camera trap* is a _____.

B. Complete the sentences according to the text.

1. Some animals that we thought were extinct have actually been *rediscovered*, or

_____.

2. In 2002, scientists were in East Africa studying *carnivores*,

_____.

3. Scientists had only seen the fish as a *fossil:*

_____.

7 | Discussing the Issues

Answer the questions and discuss your answers with a partner.

1. Which of the four animals from the text did you think was the most amazing return from extinction? Why?

2. Do you think that humans may someday be extinct? Why or why not?

Putting It On Paper

A. Write a paragraph on one of these topics.

1. How have humans caused the extinction of some animals?

2. What can governments do to protect animals?

3. Should endangered animals be kept in zoos?

Steps for your paragraph

    a. State your main idea or opinion in the first sentence; this is your topic sentence.

    b. Write three sentences with details—facts and examples that support your opinion or your main idea.

    c. Summarize your ideas in a final sentence.

B. Exchange paragraphs with a partner. Read your partner's paragraph and answer the questions in the checklist below. Give feedback to your partner.

✔ CHECKLIST
1. Can you identify the main idea or your partner's opinion?
2. Are there three examples to support the topic? Number them on the paper.
3. Does your partner give good examples or reasons? Explain below.
4. Is any of the information not related to the topic? If so, underline it on your partner's paper and then write it below.

_____

_____

_____

_____

_____

_____

C. Revise your work based on your partner's feedback.

Taking It Online | Animal Education

A. With a partner, use the Internet to research endangered animals.

1. Decide on three endangered animals that you both would like to learn about.

2. Use Google (www.google.com) or another major search engine to find sites with the information you want.

3. Preview the sites the same way you would preview a magazine article or an essay.

ONLINE TIP

Use key words to find information on a search engine:
Endangered white
    rhinoceros
Endangered shark
Endangered animals
    Brazil

B. Complete the table with the information you find.

Name of animal	Where the animal lives	Number of existing animals	Reasons for endangerment
1.			
2.			
3.			

C. Following up. Tell your classmates some facts about the most interesting endangered animal you found.

The Art of Gardening

Answer the questions and briefly discuss your answers with a partner.

1. Do you enjoy horticulture (gardening)?

2. Look at the photos and identify the items. What kinds of plants do you think will grow from them?

3. Have you ever had a garden? What did you grow?

Text 1 | Giant Pumpkins

1 | Getting Started

A. Answer the questions and briefly discuss your answers with a partner.

1. Have you ever been to a flower show or plant competition? What did you see?

2. How big is the average pumpkin?

3. How big do you think a prize-winning giant pumpkin could grow?

B. Check (✔) what is needed to grow a giant pumpkin.

☐ 1. water
☐ 2. ten acres of land
☐ 3. seeds
☐ 4. pie
☐ 5. insects
☐ 6. fertilizer
☐ 7. bulbs
☐ 8. soil

2 | Skipping Words

A. Read the following sentences. Cross out the words you do not understand. Then write their parts of speech on the blanks.

1. He grew world champion pumpkins for four consecutive years, from 1979 to 1982, and missed winning the fifth year by a mere 5 pounds.

   _____

2. I don't have any training in genetics; it was all trial and error.

   _____

3. He inherited his love of pumpkins from his father.

   _____

4. A giant pumpkin can gain 15 to 20 pounds a day, so careful watering—every day or two—is essential.

   _____

B. With a partner, discuss the parts of the sentences you do understand.

3 | Active Previewing

Preview the newspaper article on the next page by reading the first two paragraphs. Then discuss your answers with a partner.

1. Who is the article about?

2. What does he grow?

3. Where does he live?

4. When did he grow world champion pumpkins?

READING SKILL Scanning a Text

Remember that **scanning** is looking for information quickly before or after you read a text. You can **scan** for names, key words, or brief answers to questions.

To scan a text:

1. Decide what information you want to find: a date, a place, a number.

2. Predict what signal will help you: capital letters, numbers, key words.

3. Move your eyes quickly across the page—using your finger or a pencil if you wish. Look only for the information you want to find. Do not read whole sentences until you've found your answer.

4 | Scanning

Quickly scan the text on the next page for the answer to each question.

1. How many acres is Howard Dill's farm? _____

2. How many pumpkin pies were made from one giant pumpkin? _____

3. Who grew the 2006 world champion pumpkin? _____

4. How much did Howard Dill's favorite pumpkin weigh? _____

5. How many acres of Halloween pumpkins does Dill plant? _____

5 | Reading and Recalling

A. Read the text. Stop after each paragraph and tell a partner two things that you remember about it.

Gardening Giant: Howard Dill

BY CATHY CROMELL

1   Howard Dill is a giant among giant pumpkin growers. He grew world champion pumpkins for four consecutive years, from 1979 to 1982, and missed winning the fifth year by a mere 5 pounds. Today, his Dill Atlantic Giant seeds are sold worldwide to more than 50 seed companies. The pumpkins grown from his Dill Atlantic Giant seeds commonly weigh in at over 1,000 pounds. "I don't have any training in genetics; it was all trial and error[1]," Dill says. He inherited his love of pumpkins from his father and has enjoyed growing them for years.

2   Dill still grows giant pumpkins, but not for competition. In the fall, visitors come to enjoy the pumpkin patch[2] on his 90-acre farm in Nova Scotia, Canada. He plants ten acres of pumpkins for Halloween and two acres of giant pumpkins. One of his giant pumpkins was recently baked into 442 pumpkin pies and sold at $5 each for charity[3].

3   If you want to try growing a giant pumpkin, Dill recommends starting with a soil test and then adding fertilizer[4] as needed. Plant the giant pumpkin seed. A giant pumpkin can gain 15 to 20 pounds a day, so careful watering—every day or two—is essential. You should wait about 130 days until the pumpkin matures[5] and then you can harvest[6] it.

4   Dill's favorite pumpkin set the Guinness Book

record in 1981. It weighed 493.5 pounds. "I've grown them larger since, but that one meant a lot," he remembers. "I never would have predicted ten years ago that there would be a 1,000-pounder, but there are many of them now," says Dill. The 2006 world record holder is Larry Checkon of Pennsylvania. He grew a 1,469 pounder. Dill says, "These world champions are grown from my seeds, so I feel like a winner right along with them."

---

[1] **trial and error:** testing different ways to do something in order to find the best way

[2] **patch:** a small piece of land used for growing vegetables

[3] **charity:** an organization that helps people in need

[4] **fertilizer:** plant food

[5] **to mature:** to become fully grown

[6] **to harvest:** to pick the plants you have grown

B. Read the text again without pausing. Tell your partner two new pieces of information that you remember.

C. Work as a class or in large groups. Say one thing you remember about the text.

6 | Understanding the Text

A. Complete as many statements as you can without looking at the text. Discuss your answers with a partner.

1. Howard Dill is

    a. the owner of a giant pumpkin seed company.

    b. the 2006 world champion pumpkin grower.

    c. the baker who made 442 pies out of a single giant pumpkin.

2. Howard Dill inherited his love of pumpkins from

    a. his mother.

    b. his father.

    c. his grandfather.

3. Howard Dill's favorite pumpkin set the world record in

    a. 1979.

    b. 1981.

    c. 2006.

4. Howard Dill's farm is located in

    a. Pennsylvania.

    b. Nebraska.

    c. Nova Scotia.

5. Now, Howard grows _____ acres of giant pumpkins on his farm.

    a. two

    b. ten

    c. 90

B. Without looking at the text, put the instructions for growing a giant pumpkin in order from first (1) to last (6).

_____ a. Water regularly.

_____ b. Wait 130 days for it to mature.

_____ c. Test your soil.

_____ d. Plant the giant pumpkin seed.

_____ e. Harvest the giant pumpkin.

_____ f. Add fertilizer.

7 | Discussing the Issues

Answer the questions and discuss your answers with a partner.

1. Why does Howard Dill feel like a winner when other people's pumpkins win world records?

2. What other fruits and vegetables do you think are grown for competitions?

3. Would you like to try growing a giant pumpkin? Why or why not?

Text 2 | The Garden on Robben Island

1 | Getting Started

Look at the photo and then answer the questions. Briefly discuss your answers with a partner.

1. Who is Nelson Mandela?

2. Why was he in prison?

3. How long was he in prison?

4. What activities do you think Mandela enjoyed while in prison?

2 | Skipping Words

A. Read the following sentences. Cross out the words you do not understand. Then write their parts of speech on the blanks.

1. In order to start my garden, I had to excavate a great many rocks to allow the plants room to grow. _____

2. To plant a seed, watch it grow, to tend it and then harvest it, offered a simple but enduring satisfaction. _____

3. The sense of being the custodian of this small patch of earth offered a small taste of freedom. _____

4. In some ways, I saw the garden as a metaphor for certain aspects of my life.

_____

B. With a partner, discuss the parts of the sentences you do understand.

3 | Active Previewing

Preview the academic text below. Underline the title, the author, the first sentence of each paragraph, and the last sentence of the text as you preview. Then answer these questions with a partner.

1. Whose autobiography is this?

2. What is the text about?

4 | Reading and Recalling

A. Read the text. Stop after each paragraph and tell a partner two things that you remember about it.

Mandela's Garden

by Nelson Mandela

1   Almost from the beginning of my sentence[1] on Robben Island, I asked the authorities for permission to start a garden in the courtyard. For years, they refused without offering a reason. But eventually they agreed, and we were able to cut out a small garden on a narrow patch of earth against the far wall.

2   The soil in the courtyard was dry and rocky. The courtyard had been constructed over a landfill[2], and in order to start my garden, I had to excavate a great many rocks to allow the plants room to grow. At the time, some of my comrades[3] joked with me. They said that I was a miner[4] at heart, for I spent my days at the quarry[5] and my free time digging in the courtyard.

3   While I have always enjoyed gardening, it was not until I was behind bars that I was able to tend my own garden. I began to order books on gardening and horticulture. I studied different gardening techniques and types of fertilizer. I did not have many of the materials that the books discussed, but I learned through trial and error. For a time, I attempted to grow peanuts, and used different soils and fertilizers for them, but I finally gave up. It was one of my only failures.

continued

---

[1] **sentence:** the time a prisoner is in prison

[2] **landfill:** an outdoor area where trash is buried

[3] **comrades:** friends

[4] **miner:** a person who works underground in a mine digging (for coal, salt, silver, etc.)

[5] **quarry:** an open pit where stone is dug

continued

4   A garden was one of the few things in prison that one could control. To plant a seed, watch it grow, to tend it and then harvest it, offered a simple but enduring satisfaction. The sense of being the custodian of this small patch of earth offered a small taste of freedom.

5   In some ways, I saw the garden as a metaphor for certain aspects of my life. A leader must also tend his garden; he, too, plants seeds, tends them, and harvests the result. Like the gardener he must mind[6] his work, try to repel[7] the enemies, preserve what can be preserved, and eliminate what cannot succeed.

[6] **mind:** pay attention to, watch
[7] **repel:** force something to go away

B. Read the text again without pausing. Tell your partner two new pieces of information that you remember.

C. Work as a class or in large groups. Say one thing you remember about the text.

5 | Understanding the Text

A. Without looking at the text, write *T* for *True* and *F* for *False*. Discuss your answers with a partner.

_____ **1.** Nelson Mandela worked in a quarry during the day.

_____ **2.** Mandela had many gardens before coming to Robben Island.

_____ **3.** Mandela read books on gardening to learn more about it.

_____ **4.** Mandela grew peanuts successfully.

_____ **5.** Mandela found gardening very satisfying.

B. Circle the best answers to complete the statements. Discuss your answers with a partner.

1. The garden was

    a. in the quarry on the rocks.

    b. in the courtyard near the wall.

    c. on the prison roof.

2. Mandela ordered books on

    a. horticulture.

    b. mining.

    c. rocks.

3. To give room for his plants to grow, Mandela had to

    a. tear down the courtyard.

    b. ask for a larger space.

    c. dig up rocks.

4. For Mandela, gardening was satisfying because

    a. it gave him something to do.

    b. it was good exercise.

    c. it gave him a feeling of freedom.

5. Mandela compares being a gardener with being

    a. a student.

    b. a leader.

    c. a prisoner.

 VOCABULARY STRATEGY Understanding Subject and Object Pronouns

Pronouns refer to nouns. We use pronouns to avoid repeating the same nouns over and over again. Usually, a pronoun refers to the closest and/or most logical noun (or pronoun) near it in a sentence or paragraph.

A **subject pronoun** is used as the subject of a sentence or clause. The subject pronouns are: **I, you, he, she, it, we, you,** and **they**.

Read the following examples.

1. I asked the authorities for permission to start a garden in the courtyard. For years, *they* refused without offering a reason.

The authorities is the nearest and the most logical noun that comes before *they* in the paragraph. Therefore, *they* refers to *the authorities*.

2. When *he* was in his garden, Mandela felt satisfied.

The pronoun *he* is in a dependant clause in this sentence; *he* refers to *Mandela*, which appears after the pronoun.

An **object pronoun** is used as the object of a sentence, clause, or phrase. The object pronouns are **me, you, him, her, it, us, you,** and **them.**

Read the following example.

To plant a seed, watch *it* grow …

Seed is the noun that *it* refers to.

6 | Understanding Subject and Object Pronouns

Write the subject or object that the pronoun refers to, according to the text. Discuss your answers with a partner.

1. they (they agreed) (¶1) _____

2. they (they said) (¶2) _____

3. them (for them) (¶3) _____

4. it (it was one of my only failures) (¶3) _____

5. he (he, too) (¶5) _____

6. them (tends them) (¶5) _____

7 | Discussing the Issues

Reread ¶5 in the text. Then answer the questions and discuss your answers with a partner.

1. How does Mandela think a gardener's work is like a leader's work?

2. Who or what are the enemies of a gardener? Who or what are the enemies of a leader?

3. What does a gardener want to preserve? What does a leader want to preserve?

4. What does a gardener need to eliminate? What does a leader need to eliminate?

5. Do you think this is a good metaphor? Why or why not?

Text 3 | Bulb Planting

1 | Getting Started

Answer the questions and briefly discuss your answers with a partner.

1. Have you ever planted a bulb? If so, what kind was it? Was it successful?

2. What time of year do plants bloom, or flowers grow, in your area?

3. Check (✔) all the vegetables and flowers that grow from bulbs. Guess if you aren't sure.

- [ ] a. daffodil
- [ ] b. daisy
- [ ] c. garlic
- [ ] d. lily
- [ ] e. onion
- [ ] f. orchid
- [ ] g. peanut
- [ ] h. pumpkin
- [ ] i. rose
- [ ] j. tulip

 GRAPHICS Understanding Bar Graphs

Bar graphs are a useful way to organize information. Bar graphs show information in both vertical (up and down) and horizontal (left and right) directions.

To read a bar graph:

1. Read the title.

2. Read the vertical labels. For example, in the graph on the next page, these are *Planting Depth,* and *Plant Height.* The scale is shown in inches and feet.

3. Read the information across the chart. For example, a dutch iris bulb is planted three inches below the ground and grows to about 1½ feet. It blooms in April.

2 | Active Previewing

Preview the bar graph on the next page and then answer the questions. Discuss your answers with a partner.

1. What is the title of the bar graph?

2. What information does the graph show?

3. Who do you think this graph is for?

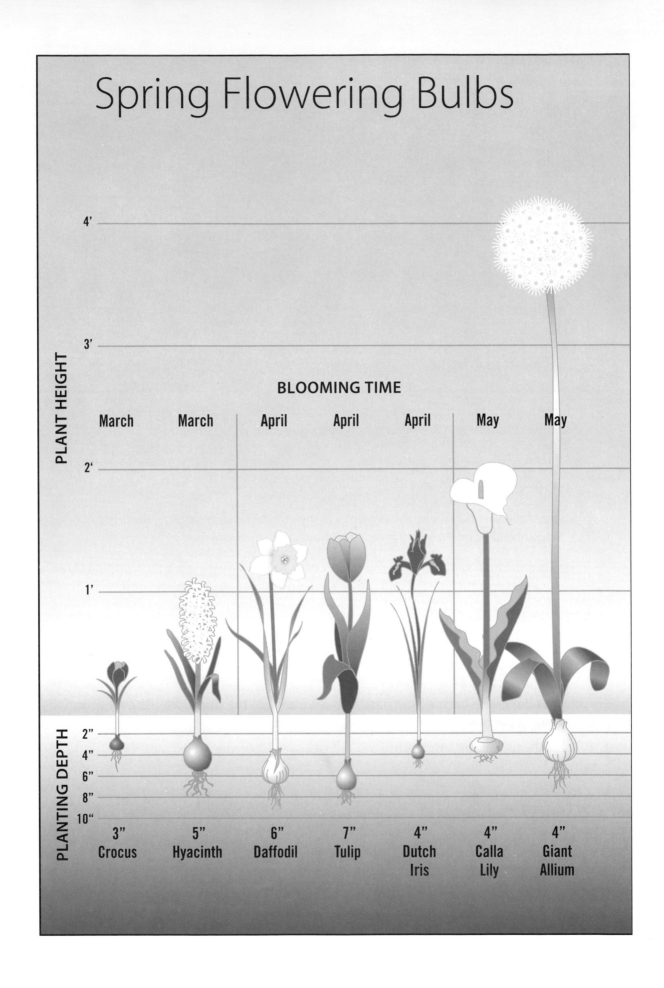

Spring Flowering Bulbs

PLANT HEIGHT

4'
3'

BLOOMING TIME

| March | March | April | April | April | May | May |

2'
1'

PLANTING DEPTH

2"
4"
6"
8"
10"

| 3" | 5" | 6" | 7" | 4" | 4" | 4" |
| Crocus | Hyacinth | Daffodil | Tulip | Dutch Iris | Calla Lily | Giant Allium |

3 | Scanning

Scan the graph for answers to the following questions. Discuss your answers with a partner.

1. How deep should you plant a daffodil bulb? How high does it grow? When will it bloom?

_____

_____

2. Which bulb should you plant the deepest? How deep should it be planted?

_____

_____

3. Which bulb grows the tallest? How tall does it grow?

_____

_____

4. Which bulb blooms the earliest? When does it bloom?

_____

_____

5. Which bulb blooms the latest? When does it bloom?

_____

_____

4 | Discussing the Issues

Answer the questions and discuss your answers with a partner.

1. According to the graph, do taller plants bloom earlier? How much deeper should gardeners plant the bulbs of taller plants than others?

2. Which of the bulbs in the graph would you want to grow?

3. Do you often give flowers to people? If so, what type of flowers do you give …

    a. … to a friend on his or her birthday?

    b. … to a boyfriend or girlfriend on a date?

    c. … to a sick friend in the hospital?

Text 4 | Orchid Obsession

1 | Getting Started

A. Look at the photo and then answer the questions. Briefly discuss your answers with a partner.

1. What is your favorite type of flower? Why?

2. Have you ever had an orchid? If so, describe it.

3. Have you ever hunted for a plant, such as a flower, berry, mushroom, herb, or tree? What did you look for?

B. Work with a partner to check your knowledge of orchids. Write _T_ if you think the statement is _True_ and _F_ if you think it is _False_.

_____ 1. There are five species of orchids.

_____ 2. Orchids only grow in warm, wet climates.

_____ 3. Orchids have the largest seed of all plants.

_____ 4. It takes five to seven years from the time of planting until the plant blooms.

_____ 5. Orchid plants can live to be 100 years old.

_____ 6. The chocolate bean comes from an orchid.

2 | Active Previewing

Preview the magazine article on the next page. Read and underline the title, the first sentence of each paragraph, and the last sentence of the text as you preview. Then answer the following questions with a partner.

1. What is the text about?

2. What do you think _orchidomania_ means?

3 | Scanning

Scan the article quickly for the numbers and words in bold to find answers to the following questions. Do not read whole sentences.

1. What year did a team of orchid hunters go to the Philippines? _____

_____

_____

2. When did John Day live? _____

_____

_____

3. Who went to Central America in the year 2000? _____

_____

_____

4 | Reading and Recalling

A. Read the text. Stop after each paragraph and tell a partner two things that you remember about it.

Orchidomania

1   Orchids have always had a reputation as an exotic and fascinating flower. To many, they represent passion and mystery. Today, common orchids are sold for as little as $10 at supermarkets and flower shops. But orchids were not always so inexpensive or common. Many people have risked their lives to discover and collect rare varieties of orchids. Orchidomania, a strangely strong interest in orchids, is as common today as it was in the past.

2   Until recently, orchid collecting was a pastime, or hobby, only for the very prosperous—only the rich could afford to buy an orchid. Orchids were usually found in faraway, remote locations and were hard to grow in colder climates. In the 1830s, an English botanist[1], Dr. Nathaniel Ward, made a glass container to transport plants long distances.

continued

------
[1] **botanist:** a person who studies plants

continued

Finally, it became possible for orchid collectors to bring home their treasured (or loved) plants. From that time, the orchid's popularity increased in England.

3   Orchid hunters were hired to travel to distant countries and bring back exotic new species. The hunters returned to Europe with thousands of orchids. They also brought with them tales of adventure. Benedict Roezl was a famous Czech orchid hunter. He discovered 800 new species of orchid from around the world. Another famous orchid grower and hunter, an Englishman named John Day, discovered many varieties and painted thousands of pictures of his beautiful finds.

> **Orchid hunters were hired to travel to distant countries and bring back exotic new species.**

4   Not all expeditions—or journeys—were successful, however. In 1908, a team of eight orchid hunters went on an expedition to the Philippine Islands. Reports say that one died of a tiger attack, another at the hands of natives (the people of that area were headhunters), and several more died in accidents and illness. Only one orchid hunter left the island. He carried with him 47,000 orchids.

5   Many orchids today are mass-produced—grown in large amounts in big, controlled areas. For many people, however, orchid hunting is still an obsession[2]. And it is still a dangerous pastime. In 2000, Tom Hart-Dyke, a young British horticulturalist, went to Central America. He was looking for a new orchid species to name after his grandmother. He was kidnapped and held captive for nine months by guerrillas—a military group fighting against the government. When asked at a press conference whether the trip to the dangerous area had been unwise, Hart-Dyke smiled and answered, "No comment."

6   To many, the passion of orchid hunters seems extreme. It is because of this passion throughout history, however, that the beautiful orchid is now easily accessible, available for all to enjoy.

---

[2] **obsession:** an interest that you think about all the time

B. Read the text again without pausing. Tell your partner two new pieces of information that you remember.

C. Work as a class or in large groups. Say one thing you remember about the text.

5 | Understanding the Text

A. Without looking at the text, circle the best answer to complete as many statements as you can. Discuss your answers with a partner.

1. In the past, orchids were

    a. only for very wealthy people.

    b. available to everybody.

    c. not very popular.

2. Before the 1830s, orchid hunters were unable to

    a. travel to remote locations.

    b. grow orchids from seeds.

    c. transport their orchids home.

3. Orchid hunters of the 1800s were mostly from

    a. the Philippines.

    b. Africa.

    c. Europe.

4. One of the most tragic orchid-hunting expeditions occurred in

    a. 1830.

    b. 1908.

    c. 2000.

5. Today, common orchid species are

    a. mass-produced.

    b. from the Philippines.

    c. highly expensive.

6. In 2000, Tom Hart-Dyke was looking for a new orchid species to name after his

    a. mother.

    b. sister.

    c. grandmother.

B. Fill in the chart according to the text. Discuss your answers with a partner.

Name	Where was he from?	When did he live?	What did he do?
1. Nathaniel Ward			
2. Benedict Roezl			
3. John Day			
4. Tom Hart-Dyke			

6 | Understanding Subject Pronouns

Write the noun that the pronoun refers to, according to the text.

1. they (they represent) (¶1) _____

2. they (they also brought) (¶3) _____

3. he (he discovered) (¶3) _____

4. he (he carried with him) (¶4) _____

5. it (it is still) (¶5) _____

6. he (he was looking for a new) (¶5) _____

One strategy for understanding unknown words is to look for **synonyms**. Synonyms are words that have the same or a similar meaning. Sometimes synonyms of unknown words can be found following a comma (,) or a dash (—), or within parentheses ( ).

Read the following sentences.

1. Until recently, orchid collecting was a pastime, or hobby, only for the very prosperous. (¶2)

What does *pastime* mean?

The comma + *or* shows that *pastime* means *hobby*.

2. Finally, it became possible for orchid collectors to bring home their treasured (or loved) plants. (¶2)

What does *treasured* mean?

The information in parentheses ( ) tells us that *treasured* means *loved*.

3. Not all expeditions—or journeys—were successful, however. (¶4)

What is an *expedition*?

The information set off by dashes (—) shows that an expedition is a journey, in this case, for orchid hunting.

7 | Understanding Vocabulary in Context—Synonyms and Definitions

Read the following sentences. Circle the part of speech for the underlined words. Then write a synonym or definition for each.

1. <u>Orchids</u> have always had a reputation as an exotic and facinating flower.

☐ a. noun   ☐ b. verb   ☐ c. adjective

_____

2. Orchids have always had a reputation as an <u>exotic</u> and facinating flower.

☐ a. noun   ☐ b. verb   ☐ c. adjective

_____

3. <u>Orchidomania</u>, a strangely strong intrest in orchids, is as common today as it was in the past.

☐ a. noun   ☐ b. verb   ☐ c. adjective

_____

4. Until recently, orchid collecting was a pastime, or hobby, only for the very <u>prosperous</u>—only the rich could afford to buy an orchid.

☐ a. noun ☐ b. verb ☐ c. adjective

---

5. Orchids were usually found in faraway, <u>remote</u> locations and were hard to grow in colder climates.

☐ a. noun ☐ b. verb ☐ c. adjective

---

6. Reports say that one died of a tiger attack, another at the hands of <u>natives</u> (the people of that area were headhunters), and several more died in accidents and illness.

☐ a. noun ☐ b. verb ☐ c. adjective

---

7. Many orchids today are <u>mass-produced</u>—grown in large amounts in big, controlled areas.

☐ a. noun ☐ b. verb ☐ c. adjective

---

8. It is because of this passion throughout history, however, that the beautiful orchid is now easily <u>accessible</u>, available for all to enjoy.

☐ a. noun ☐ b. verb ☐ c. adjective

---

8 | Discussing the Issues

Answer the questions and briefly discuss your answers with a partner.

1. What are some reasons why orchids were so expensive in the 1800s? Why are they less expensive now?

2. Would you like to go on an orchid-hunting trip? Where do you think would be a good place to hunt for new orchid species?

3. Do you think some orchid species may be endangered? Why?

Putting It On Paper

A. Write a paragraph on one of these topics.

1. Would you prefer to have a flower garden or a vegetable garden? Why?

2. Should children be required to learn horticulture in school? Why or why not?

3. Should people in prison be allowed to have gardens? Why or why not?

Steps for your paragraph

a. State your opinion in the first sentence; this is your topic sentence.

b. Write three sentences with details—facts and examples that support your opinion.

c. Summarize your ideas in a final sentence.

B. Exchange paragraphs with a partner. Read your partner's paragraph and answer the questions in the checklist. Give feedback to your partner.

✔ CHECKLIST
1. Is your partner's opinion clear?
2. Are there three examples to support the topic? Number them on the paper.
3. Does your partner give good examples or reasons? Explain below.
4. Is any of the information not related to the topic? If so, underline it on your partner's paper and then write it below.

_____

_____

_____

_____

_____

_____

C. Revise your work based on your partner's feedback.

Taking It Online | Gardening

A. With a partner, use the Internet to research gardening.

1. Decide on three plants that you both would like to grow in a garden.

2. Use Google (www.google.com) or another major search engine to find sites with the information you want.

3. Preview the sites the same way you would preview a magazine article or an essay.

ONLINE TIP

Use key words to find information on a search engine:

tulips planting
  information
how to grow giant
  pumpkin seeds
growing flowers &
  desert climate

B. Complete the table with the information you find.

Type of plant	Best location to grow	Best time to plant	Plant height
1.			
2.			
3.			

C. **Following up.** Tell your classmates about your favorite plants to grow. Explain your choices.

4 # Competition

Answer the questions and briefly discuss your answers with a partner.

1. Do you like to participate in sports?

2. Identify the sports in the photos. Have you ever participated in any of them?

3. Which sports do you like to play? Which sports do you like to watch?

Text 1 | A Three-in-One Sport

1 | Getting Started

A. Answer the questions and briefly discuss your answers with a partner.

1. What are some examples of difficult athletic competition for individuals?

2. What is a triathlon? Which three sports does it consist of?

3. Have you ever participated in or watched a triathlon?

B. How do you think triathletes prepare themselves for a race? Check (✔) the activities they might do.

☐ 1. ask for help from friends
☐ 2. bike, swim, and run
☐ 3. do yoga
☐ 4. drink lots of water
☐ 5. get massages regularly
☐ 6. have good nutrition
☐ 7. lift weights
☐ 8. sleep at high altitudes
☐ 9. set a goal
☐ 10. sleep 8 hours each night
☐ 11. watch athletics on TV

2 | Active Previewing

Preview the online article on the next page. Underline the title, the first sentence of each paragraph, and the last sentence of the text as you preview. Then answer the following questions with a partner.

1. What is the text about?

2. When and where is the Ironman held?

3 | Scanning

Quickly scan the text on the next page to find the answers to these questions.

1. How long is the ocean swim? _____

2. What time does the competition begin? _____

3. How many hours a week does an athlete usually train for the Ironman? _____

A. Read the text. Stop after each paragraph and tell a partner two things that you remember about it.

The Ironman

1   Each October, about 1,800 male and female athletes come from all over the world to compete. They are competitors in a challenging triathlon called the Ironman. The competition is a combination of three types of races. Athletes start with a 2.4-mile ocean swim. Then they get on bicycles for a 112-mile bike race. They finish the triathlon by running a marathon—a 26.2-mile foot race. The competition begins at 7 a.m. The athletes who cross the finish line by midnight are called Ironmen.

2   So how does a competitor train for this ultimate race? Most triathletes begin training months before the race. They increase their endurance—their ability to perform for a long period of time—through daily biking, running, and swimming. Many competitors add weight lifting, yoga, and/or Pilates to their routines[1]. The average Ironman triathlete spends 18–24 hours each week training for this event.

3   Good nutrition, or healthy eating, is also an important part of preparing for this difficult race. Eating high-quality food provides fuel to push the body to do its best. During the race, triathletes drink water and sports drinks. Many also eat soup, fruit, or a specially designed energy gel.

4   Getting ready for the Ironman involves preparation of the mind as well as the body. Most athletes begin their training by setting an objective, or goal. For some, the objective is to win. Others want to improve their time. Some simply want to finish the race. These Ironman competitors develop training plans. They ask for the support of friends, family, and coworkers. As they train, many athletes imagine themselves on race day, crossing the finish line.

5   The Ironman triathlon is probably the most difficult athletic event ever created. To most people, the idea of such a competition sounds insane—a person must be crazy to attempt such a difficult race. To a few athletes, however, the Ironman race is the ultimate athletic challenge. These people spend an enormous[2] amount of time in training their bodies and minds, all for the title "Ironman."

---

[1] **routines**: scheduled training
[2] **enormous**: large

B. Read the text again without pausing. Tell your partner two new pieces of information that you remember.

C. Work as a class or in large groups. Say one thing you remember about the text.

5 | Understanding the Text

A. Answer as many questions as you can without looking at the text. Discuss your answers with a partner.

1. What must an athlete do to be called an "Ironman"?

   a. finish the competition

   b. finish the competition by midnight

   c. win the competition

2. How long is a marathon?

   a. 2.4 miles

   b. 112 miles

   c. 26.2 miles

3. What do all Ironman athletes include in their training?

   a. biking, swimming, and running

   b. relaxation, meditation, and high-protein diets

   c. drinking water and sports drinks

4. What do Ironman triathletes usually eat and/or drink during the race?

   a. only water

   b. water, sports drinks, soup, and bananas

   c. water and a variety of high-quality foods

5. According to the text, how do most triathletes start their training?

   a. by setting a goal

   b. by winning other races

   c. by buying new running shoes

B. Write _T_ for _True_ and _F_ for _False_ according to the text. Discuss your answers with a partner.

_____ 1. The Ironman is held each year in California.

_____ 2. The Ironman competition is a triathlon.

_____ 3. Ironman competitors usually train 5–10 hours per week.

_____ 4. The Ironman competition is only for men.

_____ 5. The Ironman is probably the most difficult athletic competition in the world.

READING SKILL Understanding the Topic

The **topic** is the subject of a text or a paragraph. You can state the topic in just a word or a phrase, not a complete sentence.

To identify the topic:

1. Think of a word or phrase that most closely describes the subject of the *whole* paragraph or text.

2. Reread the text to make sure that the topic is not too general or too specific.

Reread ¶**3** on page 59 and choose the best topic:

    a. food

    b. sports drinks while racing

    c. nutrition for the Ironman

Choice *a* is too general. It does not include anything about the Ironman competition.

Choice *b* is too specific. It is only one detail in the paragraph.

Choice *c* is the best topic for ¶**3**.

6 | Understanding the Topic

A. Text. Answer the following questions. Write *T* for *Topic*, *G* for *Too General*, and *S* for *Too Specific*. Discuss your answers with a partner.

1. What is the topic of the text?

    a. _____ competing in difficult athletic events

    b. _____ training for the Ironman

    c. _____ setting training objectives for the Ironman

2. Is your answer for the topic here the same as your answer in *Active Previewing* on page 58?

B. Paragraphs. Answer the following questions. Write *T* for *Topic*, *G* for *Too General*, and *S* for *Too Specific*. Discuss your answers with a partner.

1. What is the topic for ¶**1**?

    a. _____ the Ironman competition

    b. _____ triathlons

    c. _____ a 2.4-mile ocean swim

2. What is the topic for ¶**2**?

    a. _____ average weekly training times

    b. _____ training the body for the Ironman

    c. _____ getting fit

3. What is the topic for ¶4?

    a. _____ getting motivated

    b. _____ asking for support from friends

    c. _____ training the mind for competition

7 | Understanding Vocabulary in Context—Definitions

Write a definition for each word below. Look back at the text on page 59 for help.

1. marathon _____

2. endurance _____

3. nutrition _____

4. objective _____

5. insane _____

> **REMEMBER**
> Sometimes, you can find the definition of a word or phrase within the same sentence.

8 | Discussing the Issues

Answer the questions and discuss your answers with a partner.

1. Which part of a triathlon (running, swimming, or biking) are you the best at?

2. Would you ever want to compete in an Ironman?

3. Are there any dangers to a competition like the Ironman? Explain.

Text 2 | Athletes in Training

1 | Getting Started

A. Answer the questions and briefly discuss your answers with a partner.

1. Do you try to keep fit? If so, how?

2. How do world-class athletes usually train for competition?

3. Have you heard of any unusual training methods?

B. For each training activity in the chart, check (✔) whether you think it won't help, may help, or would definitely help an athlete win a competition.

Training activity	Won't help	Might help	Will help
1. eating raw eggs	☐	☐	☐
2. observing animals jump	☐	☐	☐
3. running through crowds	☐	☐	☐
4. running up and down stairs	☐	☐	☐
5. sleeping in a low-oxygen tent	☐	☐	☐
6. sleeping in the cold	☐	☐	☐
7. wearing shorts in winter	☐	☐	☐
8. working on a farm	☐	☐	☐

2 | Active Previewing

Preview the magazine article on the next page. Underline the title, the headings, and the first sentence of each paragraph as you preview. Then answer the following questions with a partner:

1. What is the text about?

2. What four athletes are discussed in this text?

3 | Scanning

Quickly scan the text on the next page for information to complete the chart. Discuss your answers with a partner.

Name	Nationality	Sport
1.	American	swimming
2.		relay running, triple and long jump
3.	Czech	
4. Tegla Loroupe		

A. Read the text. Stop after each paragraph and tell a partner two things that you remember about it.

The Strange Training Methods of World-Class Athletes

1 World-class athletes have always looked for ways to improve their level of fitness and get an edge on their competitors. During Greek and Roman times, some athletes would lift rocks and drink strange potions[1] as part of their training. In the past century, athletes have tried everything from eating raw eggs to sleeping in hyperbaric chambers[2] to have an advantage and win a competition. Here are four world-class athletes and the uncommon techniques they used to train for their competitions.

> [Nambu] observed, or closely watched, frogs and monkeys as they jumped and tried to use their techniques in his own jumps.

2 Chuchei Nambu

Chuchei Nambu was an Olympic athlete in the 1928 and 1932 games. He ran one leg, or part, of Japan's 4x100m relay (a race run by four athletes, one after the other), and he won medals[3] for the long jump and triple jump. Because Nambu lived in northern Japan, he was unable to practice outdoors in the cold winters. He trained by doing workouts in a local department store, running up and down stairs and through the crowds. Nambu also studied the natural world to improve his technique. He observed, or closely watched, frogs and monkeys as they jumped and tried to use their techniques in his own jumps.

3 Tegla Loroupe

Tegla Loroupe is an Olympic runner from Kenya. Before she won the New York City Marathon in 1994, she was unknown in the international running scene. Loroupe began running as a way to get to her school, six miles away. If she was late for school, she was punished. She also ran at home on her family's farm. Her family owned cattle, and Loroupe had to run to herd them, or control their movement as a group. At 4'11" and 90 lbs, she is still considered the fastest female marathon runner.

4 Katerina Neumannova

Katerina Neumannova is a cross-country skier from the Czech Republic. She won a gold metal in the 2006 Winter Olympics. While other athletes are in bed, Katerina Neumannova is training. Part of her training is sleeping inside a special tent. The conditions inside the tent simulate the conditions at high altitudes, like on high mountains—cold temperatures and less oxygen. Living at high altitudes allows your body to adjust[4] to less oxygen. Many people believe this improves athletic performance. Katerina has another hypoxic (low-oxygen) tent that is big enough for her to move around in. Three times each week, Katerina exercises inside her training tent.

5 Lynne Cox

Lynne Cox was the first person to swim across the Bering Strait from Alaska to Siberia. She wore only a bathing suit and swim cap. Cox began training for open-water swimming as a teenager by acclimating[5] her body to cold temperatures. She swam in cold water, slept without blankets and with the windows open, and always wore light clothes in the winter. Her techniques worked. At age 15, she became the fastest person to swim across the English Channel.

---

[1] **potion:** a liquid believed to have medical or magical powers

[2] **hyperbaric chamber:** a large, high-pressure, high-oxygen tube

[3] **medal:** a special decorative coin given as an award in competitions

[4] **adjust:** to change to fit new circumstances

[5] **acclimate:** to get used to something

B. Read the text again without pausing. Tell your partner two new pieces of information that you remember.

C. Work as a class or in large groups. Try to say as many things as you remember about the text.

5 | Understanding the Text

A. Write the name of the athlete below each picture according to the text. Discuss your answers with a partner.

1. _____ 2. _____

3. _____ 4. _____

B. Check (✔) the correct answers according to the text. Each item may be true for more than one athlete. Discuss your answers with a partner.

This athlete ...	Lynne Cox	Tegla Laroupe	Chuchei Nambu	Katerina Neumannova
1. ... (has) competed in the cold.	☐	☐	☐	☐
2. ... is/was a runner.	☐	☐	☐	☐
3. ... (has) competed in the Olympics.	☐	☐	☐	☐
4. ... usually trains/ trained indoors.	☐	☐	☐	☐
5. ... prepares/ prepared for competition while sleeping.	☐	☐	☐	☐

6 | Understanding the Topic

A. Text. Answer the following questions. Write *T* for *Topic*, *G* for *Too General*, and *S* for *Too Specific*. Discuss your answers with a partner.

1. What is the topic of the text?

   a. _____ unusual athletic training techniques

   b. _____ athletes from around the world

   c. _____ sleeping in low-oxygen tents

2. Is your answer for the topic here the same as your answer in *Active Previewing* on page 63?

B. Paragraphs. Answer the following questions. Write *T* for *Topic*, *G* for *Too General*, and *S* for *Too Specific*. Discuss your answers with a partner.

1. What is the topic for ¶1?

   a. _____ the history of sports

   b. _____ how to train in Japan in the winter

   c. _____ Chuchei Nambu's strange training methods

2. What is the topic for ¶2?

    a. _____ Tegla Laroupe's athletic career

    b. _____ Tegla Laroupe's early training

    c. _____ Tegla Laroupe's work on her family's farm

3. What is the topic for ¶3?

    a. _____ the low-oxygen environment of high altitudes

    b. _____ Katerina Neumannova's low-oxygen training

    c. _____ some famous cross-country skiers from the past

7 | Understanding Vocabulary in Context—Definitions

Write a definition for each word according to the text. Discuss your answers with a partner.

1. leg _____

2. relay _____

3. observed _____

4. herd _____

5. hypoxic _____

8 | Discussing the Issues

Answer the questions and discuss your answers with a partner.

1. If you were a world-class athlete, would you use any of the training techniques you read about in this article?

2. What other special techniques, diets, or exercises do athletes use to train? Which do you think are the most successful?

3. Are there any training techniques that are unfair for athletes to use? Why or why not?

Text 3 | Marathon Times

1 | Getting Started

A. Check (✔) the sports that are traditionally men's sports, women's sports, or both. Briefly discuss your answers with a partner.

Sport	Men's sport	Women's sport	Both
1. basketball	☐	☐	☐
2. football (American)	☐	☐	☐
3. gymnastics	☐	☐	☐
4. long-distance running	☐	☐	☐
5. short-distance running	☐	☐	☐
6. skiing	☐	☐	☐
7. soccer	☐	☐	☐
8. swimming	☐	☐	☐
9. tennis	☐	☐	☐
10. wrestling	☐	☐	☐

B. Look at the photo and then answer the questions on the next page. Briefly discuss your answers with a partner.

The New York City Marathon

1. Have you ever run a race? What kind of race was it?

2. Have you, or has someone you know, ever run a marathon? Where and when?

3. How long do you think it takes to run a marathon?

 GRAPHICS Understanding Line Graphs

A line graph is a way to show large amounts of information. Line graphs are often used to show changes over time.

To read a line graph:

1. Read the title.

2. Read the labels on the vertical axis (side) of the chart and the horizontal axis.

3. Notice the increments—the distance between each number on the axis.

4. Read the information in the chart. Look for a trend, or pattern. Does the line increase, decrease, or plateau (stay the same)?

Look at the line graph on the next page. Notice the title, "Record Marathon Times," and the labels "Year" and "Time." Time is divided in 15-minute increments and years are divided in 10-year increments. Finally, look at the information within the chart: the lines representing men's marathon times and women's marathon times.

2 | Active Previewing

Preview the line graph on the next page and then answer the questions. Discuss your answers with a partner.

1. What is the title of the graph? _____

2. What do the two lines on the graph represent? _____

_____

3. With what year does this graph begin? With what year does it end? _____

_____

RECORD MARATHON TIMES

The marathon is a 26.2-mile running race. The first modern marathon was run in the 1896 Olympics. For many years, people thought that women were not able to run a marathon. Several women secretly ran in the races, but their scores were never officially recorded. In 1971, women were finally allowed to compete in the New York City Marathon. In 1984, they were allowed to compete in the Olympics. Below is a line graph showing the record times for men and women marathon runners.

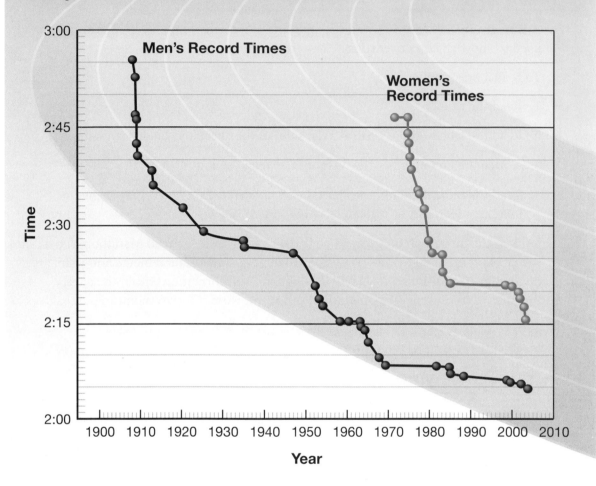

3 | Scanning

A. Scan the graph to find the answers to the questions in three minutes or less. Then discuss your answers with a partner.

1. What was the record time for men in 1970? _____

2. What was the record time for women in 2005? _____

3. In what year was the first women's marathon time recorded? _____

4. What was the difference between men's and women's record times in 1972?

   _____

5. What was the difference between men's and women's record times in 2005?

   _____

B. Using the information in the line graph, circle the best answers to complete the statements.

1. Men's record marathon times show a(n) _____ between 1910 and 1920.

   a. increase

   b. decrease

   c. plateau

2. Women's record marathon times show a(n) _____ between 1990 and 1995.

   a. increase

   b. decrease

   c. plateau

3. Between 1971 and 1985, women's marathon times show a sharp _____.

   a. increase

   b. decrease

   c. plateau

4. Between 1908 and 1912, men's marathon times show a _____.

   a. sharp decrease

   b. slight decrease

   c. sharp increase

4 | Understanding Vocabulary in Context—Synonyms

Choose the best synonym for each word. Write it on the lines below.

1. axis _____

   a. side

   b. graph

   c. information

2. increments _____

   a. the number of lines on the graph

   b. the total amount of time represented in the graph

   c. the distance between numbers on either axis

3. trend _____

   a. record   b. pattern   c. numbers

4. increase _____

   a. go down   b. go up   c. stay the same

> **REMEMBER**
>
> Synonyms are words that have the same or a similar meaning. For more on *synonyms*, see page 53.

5. decrease _____

    a. go down   b. go up   c. stay the same

6. plateau _____

    a. go down   b. go up   c. stay the same

5 | Discussing the Issues

Answer the questions and discuss your answers with a partner.

1. Do you think that women's record marathon times will ever be faster than men's?

2. Look back at the chart in *Getting Started*. Which of the traditionally men's sports are becoming more open to women?

3. Do you think men and women should be able to compete together on the same sports teams or should men's and women's teams be separate?

Text 4 | Special Olympics

1 | Getting Started

Answer the questions and briefly discuss your answers with a partner.

1. Think about a sport you enjoy. Check (✔) the **three** most important reasons that you like the sport.

    ☐ a. Competition is exciting.

    ☐ b. It's fun to play.

    ☐ c. You're successful at it.

    ☐ d. Winning builds your confidence.

    ☐ e. Sports training improves your athletic skills.

    ☐ f. You want to be a professional athlete.

    ☐ g. You want to keep fit.

    ☐ h. You want to have respect.

    ☐ i. You enjoy being with your friends and teammates.

2. Check (✔) the words and phrases that traditionally describe an athlete.

☐ a. blind

☐ b. competitive

☐ c. confident

☐ d. hard-working

☐ e. healthy

☐ f. intelligent

☐ g. old

☐ h. physically disabled

☐ i. socially skilled

☐ j. strong

☐ k. young

3. Do you think that people who do not fit the traditional model of an athlete can still be competitive in their sports?

2 | Active Previewing

Preview the newspaper article on the next page by reading the first two paragraphs. Then answer these questions. Discuss your answers with a partner.

1. Who participates in the Special Olympics?

2. Where do participants come from?

3. What did researchers find?

4. When was the research conducted?

3 | Scanning

Scan the text on the next page to find the answers to the questions. Then compare your answers with a partner.

1. How many different sports are offered in the Special Olympics? _____

2. What university were the researchers from? _____

3. What percentage of Special Olympic participants hold jobs? _____

A. Read the text. Stop after each paragraph and tell a partner two things that you remember about it.

Research Shows Benefits of Special Olympics

1   Special Olympics is a program that helps people with intellectual disabilities participate in sports. More than two million athletes are a part of this program. Special Olympics offers year-round training and competition in 26 different sports. These athletes are all ages and come from 150 different countries around the world.

2   Recently, researchers from the University of Massachusetts in Boston and the University of Utah studied the program's effect[1] on more than 2,000 athletes in the United States. The study was conducted in 2004 and 2005. Researchers found that there are many benefits[2] to being in the Special Olympics.

3   The researchers asked families, coaches[3], and athletes about the program. They found that most people saw a lot of improvement in the athletes. Because of their participation, Special Olympics athletes have better health. They also have more self-confidence and more social skills.

4   This study shows that Special Olympics gives disabled people a chance to be successful at sports. It also suggests that the improvements can go beyond sports. For example, 52 percent of adult Special Olympics athletes have jobs, but only 10 percent of non-athletes with the same disabilities have jobs. This suggests that being in Special Olympics increases a person's ability to have a job.

5   The recent research also shows that Special Olympics athletes have a lot in common with other athletes. For example, Special Olympics athletes like the social experiences in sports. Teammates often become good friends. More than half of the athletes meet their teammates outside of sports. Like other athletes, Special Olympics athletes play sports because they like to compete. They are serious about their sports and don't want pity[4] or special treatment.

6   In general, the research shows that disabled athletes do sports for the same reasons as non-disabled athletes. Even athletes who leave Special Olympics are still pleased with their Special Olympics experience. Most would participate again if they could.

---

[1] **effect:** result

[2] **benefit:** advantage, good result

[3] **coach:** person who trains an athlete or team

[4] **pity:** a sad feeling about someone's problems

B. Read the text again without pausing. Tell your partner two new pieces of information that you remember.

C. Work as a class or in large groups. Say one thing you remember about the text.

5 | Understanding the Text

A. Without looking at the text, write _T_ for _True_ and _F_ for _False_. Discuss your answers with a partner.

_____ 1. Special Olympics athletes want pity.

_____ 2. More Special Olympics athletes have jobs than non-athletes with the same disabilities.

_____ 3. Traditional athletes and Special Olympics athletes participate in sports for different reasons.

_____ 4. Researchers studied 200 Special Olympics athletes.

_____ 5. Special Olympics is an international organization.

B. Check (✔) the benefits of Special Olympics participation according to the text. Discuss your answers with a partner.

☐ 1. improves health

☐ 2. provides the chance to be successful at sports

☐ 3. provides the chance to participate in research

☐ 4. provides the chance to travel overseas

☐ 5. increases intelligence

☐ 6. increases self-confidence

☐ 7. increases athletic skills

☐ 8. increases social skills

☐ 9. increases likeliness of getting a job

☐ 10. provides the chance to earn money as a professional athlete

6 | Understanding the Topic

A. Text. Answer the following questions. Write _T_ for _Topic_, _G_ for _Too General_, and _S_ for _Too Specific_. Discuss your answers with a partner.

1. What is the topic of the text?

a. _____ Special Olympics

b. _____ the benefits of Special Olympics

c. _____ pity for Special Olympians

2. Is your answer for the topic here the same as your answer in _Active Previewing_ on page 73?

B. **Paragraphs.** Answer the following questions. Write *T* for *Topic, G* for *Too General*, and *S* for *Too Specific*. Discuss your answers with a partner.

1. What is the topic for ¶1?

   a. _____ the Special Olympics

   b. _____ athletic competitions

   c. _____ the 26 Special Olympics sports

2. What is the topic for ¶2?

   a. _____ 2,000 Special Olympics participants

   b. _____ university research

   c. _____ research into benefits of Special Olympics

3. What is the topic for ¶4?

   a. _____ non-athletic benefits of Special Olympics

   b. _____ Special Olympic athletes at work

   c. _____ jobs

7 | Understanding Subject Pronouns

Write the noun that the pronoun refers to, according to the text on page 74.

1. they (They found) (¶3) _____

2. they (They also have) (¶3) _____

3. it (It also suggests) (¶4) _____

4. they (they like to compete) (¶5) _____

5. they (if they could) (¶6) _____

> **REMEMBER**
>
> A subject pronoun is used as the subject of a sentence or clause. For more on *subject pronouns* see page 43.

8 | Discussing the Issues

Answer the questions and discuss your answers with a partner.

1. If you were organizing a Special Olympics competition, what health and safety issues would you need to consider?

2. If your child were born with an intellectual disability, would you encourage him or her to participate in Special Olympics?

3. Look at your reasons for participating in sports on page 72. Are your reasons similar to those of Special Olympics athletes? Explain.

Putting It On Paper

A. Write a paragraph on one of these topics.

1. Do professional athletes get paid too much, too little, or the right amount? Why do you think so?

2. Should young children be encouraged to participate in competitive sports? Why or why not?

3. Should women's sports get as much attention as men's sports? Why or why not?

Steps for your paragraph

a. State your opinion in the first sentence; this is your topic sentence.

b. Write three sentences with details—facts and examples that support your opinion.

c. Summarize your ideas in a final sentence.

B. Exchange paragraphs with a partner. Read your partner's paragraph and answer the questions in the checklist. Give feedback to your partner.

✔ CHECKLIST
1. Is your partner's opinion clear?
2. Are there three examples to support the topic? Number them on the paper.
3. Does your partner give good examples or reasons? Explain below.
4. Is any of the information not related to the topic? If so, underline it on your partner's paper and then write it below.

_____

_____

_____

_____

_____

_____

C. Revise your work based on your partner's feedback.

Taking It Online | The World of Athletes

A. With a partner, use the Internet to research athletes.

1. Decide on three athletes that you are both interested in learning more about.

2. Use Google (www.google.com) or another major search engine to find sites with the information you want.

3. Preview the sites the same way you would preview a magazine article or an essay.

ONLINE TIP

Use key words to find information on a search engine.
Famous gymnasts
Michael Jordan
Training techniques

B. Take notes below with the information you find.

Athlete	Nationality	Date of birth	Sport	Training techniques
1.				
2.				
3.				

C. Following up. Tell your classmates some facts about the most interesting athlete you researched.

Chapter 5   Communication

Answer the questions and briefly discuss your answers with a partner.

1. Do you use more than one form of communication in your daily life?

2. Look at the photos. Can you name each item?

3. What do the photos have in common? How are they different?

Text 1 | Baby Sign Language

1 | Getting Started

A. Look at the photo and then answer the questions. Briefly discuss your answers with a partner.

1. Before they can speak, how do babies communicate?

2. Do you think parents have an easy time or a difficult time with the way babies communicate?

3. Look at the photo on the next page. What are the mother and baby doing?

B. Check (✔) the box that reflects your opinion. Briefly discuss your answers with a partner.

☐ **1.** Parents should raise their children the same way they themselves were raised.

☐ **2.** Parents should read books on current child-raising skills and learn to use them.

☐ **3.** Parents should do a combination of *1* and *2*.

2 | Active Previewing

Preview the newspaper article on the next page. Underline the title, the first sentence of each paragraph, and the last sentence of the text as you preview. Then answer the following question with a partner.

1. What do you think this text is about?

2. What is the most important thing the author wants you to know about the topic (the main idea)?

3 | Reading and Recalling

A. Read the text. Stop after each paragraph and tell a partner two things that you remember about it.

Baby Emma Isn't Talking Yet, But She's Saying Plenty

BY ROBIN RHODES CROWELL

1   Emma and I are sitting on the bed as our cat jumps up. Emma looks at the cat, and then, without hesitation, takes both pointer fingers[1] and brushes them against her cheeks. It's her symbol for "cat."

2   Emma is learning baby signs. Baby signs are the same idea as American Sign Language (ASL)[2], but the parents and the baby determine the signs. The actual sign doesn't matter as long as everyone in the household understands it.

3   At 12 months old, Emma is too young to communicate with words. She is just starting to utter sounds that could be words such as "hat," "hot," and "hi." But she has a whole repertoire[3] of images and ideas that she communicates to us.

4   We started teaching Emma signs when she was seven months old. The motions are the same ones most infants use instinctively[4]. We started with "more" (pointer finger to palm), "bye" (waving), and "eat" (fingers to mouth).

5   We were pleased and rewarded when at nine months Emma started telling us she wanted more to eat. She moved on to more baby signs (nap, drink, book, bird, and others). Some we taught her and some she made up on her own!

6   Our experience with baby signs has helped us understand Emma's needs. One afternoon, after she and I had finished shopping at a bookstore, I put Emma into her car seat. As I handed her toys, each one was met with an upset look and an angry roar.

7   Emma then looked up at me with her big blue eyes and put her palms together and then opened them. I knew that she wanted a book to read. I gave it to her and she was happy. How incredible that, at 12 months, she was able to tell me exactly what she wanted.

8   For Emma, life without words is not a life without language.

---

[1] **pointer fingers:** the fingers next to the thumbs, often used to point at things

[2] **American Sign Language (ASL):** a communication system of hand signs used by people with hearing disabilities

[3] **repertoire:** the total number of things one is able to do

[4] **instinctively:** naturally, without thinking or learning

B. Read the text again without pausing. Tell your partner two new pieces of information that you remember.

C. Work as a class or in large groups. Say one thing you remember about the text.

4 | Understanding the Text

Answer as many questions as you can without looking at the text. Discuss your answers with a partner.

1. Why does Emma brush her fingers against her cheeks?

   a. She has an itch.

   b. It's her symbol for "cat."

   c. She wants attention.

2. What is the difference between baby signs and American Sign Language?

   a. Baby signs are a less formal system of communicating without words.

   b. Baby signs are used by babies and parents.

   c. Both *a* and *b* are correct.

3. What words can Emma sign?

   a. She can sign all words.

   b. She can't sign any words.

   c. She can sign a few words.

4. How does Emma show that she wants to look at a book?

   a. She cries.

   b. She makes the sign for "book."

   c. She takes a book from the bookshelf.

5. Can Emma communicate more by speaking or by using signs?

   a. She uses more signs than words.

   b. She uses more words than signs.

   c. She uses signs and words equally.

6. What age was Emma when she could tell her mother exactly what she wanted?

   a. six years old

   b. two years old

   c. 12 months old

5 | Understanding Subject and Object Pronouns

Find all the pronouns in the sentences in the first column. Then write each pronoun in the correct column. Discuss your answers with a partner.

Sentences from the text	Subject pronoun(s)	Object pronoun(s)
1. Emma and I are sitting on the bed as our cat jumps up. (¶1)		
2. The actual sign doesn't matter as long as everyone in the household understands it. (¶2)		
3. But she has a whole repertoire of images and ideas that she communicates to us. (¶3)		
4. We started teaching Emma signs when she was seven months old. (¶4)		
5. We were pleased and rewarded when at nine months Emma started telling us she wanted more to eat. (¶5)		
6. Our experience with baby signs has helped us understand Emma's needs. (¶6)		
7. Emma then looked up at me with her big blue eyes and put her palms together and then opened them. (¶7)		

6 | Understanding the Topic

Answer the following question. Write *T* for *Topic*, *G* for *Too General*, and *S* for *Too Specific*. Discuss your answer with a partner.

1. What is the topic of the text?

   a. _____ babies and communication

   b. _____ words Emma knows

   c. _____ the success of baby sign language

2. Is your answer for the topic of the text the same as the one you determined after you previewed the text, or is your answer different? _____

   _____

   _____

The main idea of a text, section, or paragraph is the most important point the writer wants to express. For paragraphs, the main idea is usually the first sentence. The main idea is always expressed in a complete sentence.

To identify the main idea:

1. Look for the sentence that best expresses the most important idea of the text, section, or paragraph.

2. Reread the text to make sure that the main idea is not too general or too specific.

The topic of ¶1 on page 81 is *a sign that Emma is learning.*

Some possible choices for main idea are:

a. Emma and her mother are sitting on the bed.

b. Emma learns easily.

c. Emma knows a sign for "cat" and uses it to communicate.

Choice *a* is too specific to be a good main idea. It refers to a fact about Emma and her mother rather than an idea.

Choice *b* is too general to be a good main idea. It refers to a quality of Emma's and is not necessarily related to the topic.

Choice *c* is a good main idea. It tells us what the writer wants us to know about Emma. It relates to the topic because it mentions her use of the sign for "cat."

7 | Understanding the Main Idea

A. Text. Answer the following question. Write *MI* for *Main Idea*, *G* for *Too General*, and *S* for *Too Specific*. Discuss your answers with a partner.

1. What is the main idea of the text?

   a. _____ Babies cannot communicate in spoken language.

   b. _____ Even though babies cannot communicate in spoken language, they can be taught to communicate in baby sign language.

   c. _____ Only deaf babies should learn how to use sign language.

2. Is your answer for the main idea of the text the same as the one you determined after you previewed the text, or is your answer different? _____

_____

_____

B. Paragraphs. Answer the following questions. Write *MI* for *Main Idea, G* for *Too General,* and *S* for *Too Specific*. Discuss your answers with a partner.

1. What is the main idea of ¶**2**?

    a. _____ Sign language is difficult to learn.

    b. _____ Emma is learning a sign language for babies, which is the same idea as American Sign Language.

    c. _____ American Sign Language and baby sign language are different.

2. What is the main idea of ¶**3**?

    a. _____ Emma is just beginning to use signs to communicate.

    b. _____ Sign language is better than speaking.

    c. _____ Emma knows how to say one-syllable words.

3. What is the main idea of ¶**4**?

    a. _____ Emma began learning simple signs when she was seven months old.

    b. _____ Emma's parents took her to a school to learn sign language.

    c. _____ Emma knows how to say "bye" in sign language.

4. What is the main idea of ¶**5**, ¶**6**, and ¶**7**?

    a. _____ Emma gets upset easily.

    b. _____ When Emma signs, her parents know what she wants.

    c. _____ Emma likes to look at books.

C. Paragraphs. Look at the first sentence of each paragraph in *Text 1*. Which ones give the main idea of the paragraph? Discuss your answers with a partner.

8 | Discussing the Issues

Answer the questions and discuss your answers with a partner.

1. What are the advantages of teaching babies to sign?

2. What are some possible disadvantages?

3. If you had a baby, would you teach the baby to sign? Why or why not?

Text 2 | The Whistle Language

1 | Getting Started

A. Check (✔) how old you think each method of communication is. Discuss your answers with a partner.

Method of communication	More than 1,000 years old	Less than 1,000 years old	Less than 100 years old	Modern
1. sending smoke signals	☐	☐	☐	☐
2. sending runners or messengers	☐	☐	☐	☐
3. signaling with flags	☐	☐	☐	☐
4. whistling	☐	☐	☐	☐
5. burning fires on hilltops	☐	☐	☐	☐
6. using birds to carry messages	☐	☐	☐	☐

B. Answer the following questions. Discuss your answers with a partner.

1. How does each method of communication work?

2. What are some disadvantages or difficulties of each?

2 | Active Previewing

Preview the magazine article below. Underline the title, the first sentence of each paragraph, and the last sentence of the text. Then answer the following questions with a partner.

1. What is the topic of the text?

2. Where is the language used?

3. Who is learning the language?

3 | Reading and Recalling

A. Read the text. Stop after each paragraph and tell a partner two things that you remember about it.

Just Whistle

1   People who live in La Gomera, a small island off the coast of Africa, are starting to whistle while they work again. But these are no ordinary songs.

2   In fact, Silbo Gomero is not music at all, but a whistled language you can hear only on this hilly Spanish island. Researchers believe that Silbo Gomero first came to the island with settlers from Africa over 2,500 years ago. Residents are attempting to bring the language back to life before those who know it best, the shepherds[1], can no longer pass it on.

3   The whistled language is called Silbo from "silbar," the Spanish word for whistle. In the language, whistled sounds replace Spanish words. Sounds that are whistled higher or lower have different meanings. A Silbador, or whistler, can change the level of the whistle by using his fingers. The hilly terrain[2] of the region helps the sound travel. A Silbador can direct the sound even more by cupping the other hand like a megaphone[3].

> The whistlers can communicate more than 4,000 words.

4   Whistlers do not simply pass along information about basic needs. They can carry on whole conversations. The whistlers can communicate more than 4,000 words. However, since some words sound similar, whistlers must sometimes guess the meaning.

5   In 2000, the local government required all school children in the island's fifteen schools to learn Silbo Gomero. Students between the ages of 7 and 14 practice the whistled language for half an hour a week. As a result, they can communicate with friends who live up to two miles away.

6   As many as 70 other whistled languages exist in areas with similar terrain: Greece, Turkey, China, Vietnam, and Mexico. But researchers have only studied 12. Each one is based on the language spoken in that area. Studying these languages is an important step in maintaining their existence. Modern communications systems, especially cell phones, now threaten them. The people of La Gomera hope that by teaching children their special language in school, they can continue to pass it on to future generations.

[1] **shepherds:** people who take care of sheep
[2] **terrain:** type of land, for example, a hilly area
[3] **megaphone:** a piece of equipment that makes your voice louder

B. Read the text again without pausing. Tell your partner two new pieces of information that you remember.

C. Work as a class or in large groups. Say one thing you remember about the text.

4 | Understanding the Text

Answer as many questions as you can without looking at the text. Discuss your answers with a partner.

1. What type of terrain would you see if you visited La Gomera?

   a. rocky

   b. hilly

   c. flat

2. How do shepherds make their whistles communicate different meanings?

   a. They whistle higher or lower.

   b. They cup their hands around their mouths.

   c. They guess the meaning.

3. How far away can Silbo Gomero whistles be heard?

   a. up to two miles away

   b. across the mountains

   c. to the coast of Africa

4. Where are other whistled languages found?

   a. in many other areas of Spain

   b. in some areas with similar terrain

   c. on small islands near Africa

5. Could a whistler from La Gomera communicate with a whistler from Greece?

   a. Yes, because they both know the whistle language.

   b. Sometimes, if they whistle very clearly and slowly.

   c. No, because their spoken languages are different.

6. What two things are important in maintaining the life of Silbo Gomero?

   a. teaching children and studying whistle languages

   b. getting rid of cell phones and computers

   c. using shepherds and fisherman as teachers

5 | Understanding the Topic and Main Idea

Text. Answer the following questions. Discuss your answers with a partner.

1. What is the topic of the text?

    a. Silbo Gomero, the whistled language of La Gomera

    b. ancient types of communication in Spain

    c. modern communication systems

    d. the First International Congress of Whistled Languages

2. What is the main idea of the text?

    a. There are many whistled languages in the world.

    b. Children on La Gomera are required to learn Silbo Gomero at school.

    c. The people of La Gomera are trying to keep Silbo Gomero alive.

    d. Studying whistled languages is important in keeping them alive.

 VOCABULARY STRATEGY Understanding Vocabulary in Context—Apposition

A word or phrase that means the same as a noun and is next to that noun in the sentence is said to be in **apposition** to the noun. Words and phrases in apposition are often set off by commas. Understanding and recognizing apposition helps a reader get more information from a text.

Read the following sentence.

Shepherds, *men who take care of sheep*, are the most expert whistlers.

In this example, *men who take care of sheep* means the same thing as *shepherds*. The phrase is in apposition to *shepherds*.

A word or phrase in apposition usually further describes a noun and has the same grammatical function in the sentence. In the example above, both *shepherd* and *men who take care of sheep* are subjects.

6 | Understanding Vocabulary in Context—Apposition

Write the words in apposition according to the text. Discuss your answers with a partner.

1. La Gomera (¶1) _____

2. those who know it best (¶2) _____

7 | Discussing the Issues

Answer the questions and discuss your answers with a partner.

1. Now that more and more people have cell phones to communicate, should people try to save whistled languages? Why or why not?

2. Is it a good use of time for students on La Gomera to learn Silbo Gomero? Why or why not?

3. Can you think of any other ways to save and maintain ancient forms of communication?

Text 3 | Advances in Communication

1 | Getting Started

Answer the questions and briefly discuss your answers with a partner.

1. What are some famous inventions in the history of communication?

2. Where were these inventions created?

3. In what ways do you communicate with others?

 GRAPHICS Understanding and Previewing Timelines

Timelines appear in many different sources of information—textbooks, Websites, and many types of articles. They list events in the order they happened. Timelines can cover several hours or thousands of years.

The timeline below begins with dates B.C.E., or *before the common era*, which means before Year 1. Dates expressed as B.C.E increase as you move back in time. For example, the philosopher Aristotle was born in 384 and died in 322 B.C.E.

When there are no letters after a date, the year is C.E., or *common era*. These dates increase as you move closer to today.

To **preview** a timeline:

1. Read the title and any subtitles or bold headings.

2. Read the first date and event.

3. Read the last date and event.

2 | Active Previewing

Preview the timeline below. Then answer these questions with a partner.

1. What is the subject of the timeline?

2. What are the two eras covered by the timeline?

3. Approximately how many years does the timeline cover?

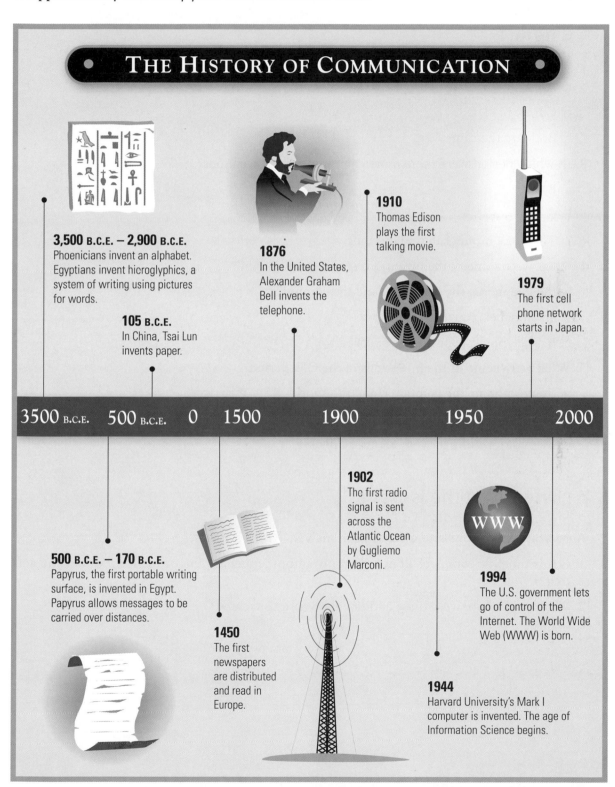

THE HISTORY OF COMMUNICATION

3,500 B.C.E. – 2,900 B.C.E.
Phoenicians invent an alphabet. Egyptians invent hicroglyphics, a system of writing using pictures for words.

105 B.C.E.
In China, Tsai Lun invents paper.

1876
In the United States, Alexander Graham Bell invents the telephone.

1910
Thomas Edison plays the first talking movie.

1979
The first cell phone network starts in Japan.

3500 B.C.E.   500 B.C.E.   0   1500   1900   1950   2000

500 B.C.E. – 170 B.C.E.
Papyrus, the first portable writing surface, is invented in Egypt. Papyrus allows messages to be carried over distances.

1450
The first newspapers are distributed and read in Europe.

1902
Thc first radio signal is sent across the Atlantic Ocean by Gugliemo Marconi.

1994
The U.S. government lets go of control of the Internet. The World Wide Web (WWW) is born.

1944
Harvard University's Mark I computer is invented. The age of Information Science begins.

3 | Understanding the Timeline

Answer as many questions as you can without looking at the timeline. Discuss your answers with a partner.

1. What is the earliest year in the timeline?

    a. 3,500 B.C.E.

    b. 500 B.C.E.

    c. 105 B.C.E.

2. Which time period is longer?

    a. B.C.E.

    b. C.E.

    c. Both are the same.

3. In which period were there more communication inventions?

    a. B.C.E.

    b. C.E.

    c. The same number in both periods.

4. What were some of the inventions of the B.C.E. period?

    a. the telephone, the telegraph, and the computer

    b. an alphabet, papyrus, and paper

    c. hieroglyphics, paper, and newspapers

5. What were some of the inventions of the C.E. period?

    a. the telephone, the computer, and the World Wide Web

    b. paper, the computer, and the World Wide Web

    c. the radio, talking movies, and the alphabet

4 | Discussing the Issues

Answer the questions and discuss your answers with a partner.

1. Is this timeline complete? If not, what inventions, either ancient or modern, would you add to it?

2. When and where were these additional inventions created?

Text 4 | Communication Technology

1 | Getting Started

Check (✔) the boxes that best describe your habits. Briefly discuss your answers with a partner.

My habits	Often	Sometimes	Never
1. I chat with family and friends in person.	☐	☐	☐
2. I write letters with pen and paper.	☐	☐	☐
3. I use a cell phone to talk with family and friends.	☐	☐	☐
4. I use e-mail to communicate, make plans, and share information.	☐	☐	☐
5. I surf the Web for information, music downloads, chat groups, etc.	☐	☐	☐
6. I use instant or text messaging.	☐	☐	☐

2 | Active Previewing

Preview the academic text on the next page. Underline the title, the first sentence of each paragraph, and the last sentence of the text as you preview. Then answer these questions. Discuss your answers with a partner.

1. What is the subject of the text?

2. Who (which two groups of people) is the text about?

3. Where is it happening?

4. When is it happening?

3 | Scanning

Scan the text quickly to complete these statements. Use the numbers and words in bold to help you. Discuss your answers with a partner.

1. **91%** of adults use _____.

2. At the company **U.S. Cellular**, employees were recently asked not to use

_____.

3. **IM** stands for _____.

> **REMEMBER**
>
> Scan, or run your finger or a pencil down the page, to look for key words, numbers, and names. See page 37 for more on *scanning a text*.

A. Read the text. Stop after each paragraph and tell a partner two things that you remember about it.

Communication in the Internet Age: Facts and Trends

1 More Americans Online Than Ever

According to a 2005 Pew survey[1], 68% of adults in the United States go online regularly, where they do a wide variety of things. Most use e-mail (91%). Many (84%) use search engines to find information. Two thirds buy products (67%). About half do job-related research. Others play online games (36%), listen to music (34%) or try to meet someone (27%).

2 Men and women use the Internet in close to equal numbers, with men going online a bit more (69%) than women (67%). Not surprisingly, younger men and women log on much more often than older adults. For example, 84% of adults between the ages of 18 and 29 use the Internet. In contrast, only 26% of adults age 65 and older log on regularly.

3 The number of teens using the Internet is even higher (87%). More teens than adults use new technologies such as Instant Messaging (IM) and text messaging in order to connect with friends. Half of all teens surveyed use the Internet daily. In the last four years, teen use of the Internet has increased by 24%.

continued

---

[1] **survey:** a set of questions to get information about people's behaviors and opinions

continued

4 Pulling the Plug to Encourage In-Person Communication

Some parents and employers are reacting to these high numbers by placing limits on Internet use. Employees at U.S. companies have to deal with three times the amount of e-mail they did in 1999. At U.S. Cellular, a Chicago-based company, workers are no longer allowed to use business-related e-mail on Fridays. The same is true at Veritas Software in Mountain View, California. There, employees can be fined $1 for sending business-related e-mail after midnight on Friday. Both companies report positive results, with more face-to-face meetings.

5   Other companies are building more common areas so that employees can sit and work together instead of staying in individual cubicles[2]. According to the Facility Performance Group, hotels are building three times more meeting spaces and conference rooms than they did 15 years ago. Americans are spending more on business travel so that they can meet in person to do business.

6   There are more and more summer camps for teenagers that advertise low-tech experiences. It is estimated that 90% of summer camps don't allow the use of cell phones or other electronic devices. Some go even further. Farm and Wilderness, a group of six camps in Vermont, has cabins[3] without electricity so that no one can go online. Campers there do not even wear watches. Instead they wait for the sound of the bell to know when it is time to move on to a new activity. Another organization, The Island School, takes young people for trips abroad to study, do volunteer work, and play sports. This school allows only one 15-minute phone call a week.

---

[2] **cubicles:** small, walled spaces for office workers within a larger room
[3] **cabins:** small, wooden houses

B. Read the text again without pausing. Tell your partner two new pieces of information that you remember.

C. Work as a class or in large groups. Say one thing you remember about the text.

5 | Understanding the Text

A. Write *T* for *True* and *F* for *False* according to the text. Discuss your answers with a partner.

_____ **1.** More adults use e-mail than search engines.

_____ **2.** Women go online more than men.

_____ **3.** Younger men and women use the Internet more often than older adults.

_____ **4.** Teens use the Internet more than any other group.

_____ **5.** Teens do not like to try new types of technology, such as IM.

B. Complete the chart according to the text. Discuss your answers with a partner.

Facts	Trends
1. 68% of American adults go online. (¶1)	1. Employers restrict Internet use. (¶4)
2.	2.
3.	3.
4.	4.
5.	5.

6 | Understanding the Main Idea

Answer the questions below. Discuss your answers with a partner.

1. What is the main idea of ¶1, ¶2, and ¶3?

_____

_____

2. What is the main idea of ¶4, ¶5, and ¶6?

_____

_____

3. What is the main idea of the text?

_____

_____

_____

7 | Discussing the Issues

Answer the questions and discuss your answers with a partner.

1. How does your use of the Internet compare with Internet use of people in the U.S. in general?

2. Do you believe that electronic communication devices and technology improve communication between people? Why or why not?

3. How would you feel about spending a week without using the Internet, phones, and other electronic devices? Explain.

Putting It On Paper

A. Write a paragraph on one of these topics.

1. What communication device would you most miss if you could no longer use it? Explain.

2. What does the future hold? Imagine a communication device that would improve people's lives and describe it. Explain why it would be useful.

3. Are we missing anything if we rely too much on technology to communicate? Explain.

Steps for your paragraph

a. State your opinion in the first sentence; this is your topic sentence.

b. Write three sentences with details—facts and examples that support your opinion.

c. Summarize your ideas in a final sentence.

B. Exchange paragraphs with a partner. Read your partner's paragraph and answer the questions in the checklist. Give feedback to your partner.

✔ CHECKLIST
1. Is your partner's opinion clear?
2. Are there three examples to support the topic? Number them on the paper.
3. Does your partner give good examples or reasons? Explain below.
4. Is any of the information not related to the topic? If so, underline it on your partner's paper and then write it below.

_____

_____

_____

_____

_____

_____

_____

C. Revise your work based on your partner's feedback.

Taking It Online | More Communication

A. With a partner, use the Internet to research a topic in communication.

1. Together, review the texts and activities in this chapter. Decide on a communication topic that you are both interested in learning more about.

2. Use Google (www.google.com) or another major search engine to find sites with the information you want. What words do you think you should type in the search box to begin your search? Write them here.

_____

3. Your search will return many "hits" (results). Preview your hits to find one text and one Website that look interesting to you.

4. Preview the sites the same way you would preview a magazine article or an essay.

> **ONLINE TIP**
>
> Add a specific place, time, or person to your search terms. For example, if you chose *Emile Berliner* as your topic, add *gramophone*. When you do a search, there is no need to use the word "and" between words.
> Emile Berliner
>   gramophone

B. Complete the table with the information you find.

Your topic:
Article title:
Article author:
Facts about communication:
Website name:
Website address:
Facts about communication:

C. Following up. What is the most interesting thing you learned about your topic? Share this with your classmates.

Natural Medicines

Answer the questions and briefly discuss your answers with a partner.

1. Do any foods that you eat change the way you feel, physically or emotionally?

2. What kinds of medical help do you think each of the photographs may represent?

3. Do you know any traditions in your own or other cultures of healing with plants?

Text 1 | International Cure

1 | Getting Started

A. Answer the questions and briefly discuss your answers with a partner.

1. Do you know anyone who has Alzheimer's disease?

2. If you do, how are they being taken care of? Are they taking any medicines?

3. What are some common symptoms of Alzheimer's disease?

4. Is it a disease that currently can be cured?

B. Check (✔) whether you agree or disagree. Briefly discuss your answers with a partner.

Statements	Agree	Disagree
1. Western medicine is the best way to treat all illnesses.	☐	☐
2. We should look around the world for ways to cure diseases.	☐	☐
3. Cures for diseases only come in pills bought at the pharmacy.	☐	☐
4. Plants are often an excellent source for new cures for diseases.	☐	☐

2 | Active Previewing

Preview the magazine article on the next page. Underline the title, the first sentence of each paragraph, and the last sentence of the text as you preview. Then answer the following question with a partner.

What do you think this text is about?

3 | Reading and Recalling

A. Read the text. Stop after each paragraph and tell a partner two things that you remember about it.

Chinese Moss May Alleviate Alzheimer's Disease

BY AMY O'CONNOR

1   A traditional Chinese herbal remedy might be effective in treating Alzheimer's disease. Experts on the disease looked at research in China and studies in the United States. Based on the results, they believe the harmless herbal remedy may be even more effective than the two drugs that doctors use now to treat the disease.

2   Alzheimer's disease affects as many as 4 million elderly Americans and 12 million people worldwide. Common symptoms[1] are dementia[2] and memory loss. There is no known cure.

3   The traditional remedy, called Qian Ceng Ta, comes from a moss[3]. It has been used for centuries in China to treat fever and inflammation[4]. The remedy has another positive effect. It slows the breakdown[5] of acetylcholine, which is a chemical in the brain that helps it work normally.

4   Alzheimer's sufferers often experience memory loss and are confused about what is happening around them. This is the result of acetylcholine breakdown. The two drugs now used to treat Alzheimer's patients improve the way the brain works. But they can also cause stomach and liver problems. Qian Ceng Ta seems to be even more effective than the drugs at treating the disease. And, it has none of the bad effects on the body.

> **Alzheimer's disease affects as many as 4 million elderly Americans and 12 million people worldwide.**

5   The traditional remedy Qian Ceng Ta has been used to treat dementia in China. Doctors there prescribe it to their patients. Reports from that country suggest that as many as 100,000 Alzheimer's patients have had their symptoms lessened, according to Alan Kozikowski, Ph.D., Georgetown University. Kozikowski first separated and studied the herbal compound in 1991.

---

[1] **symptoms:** physical signs that you have a certain illness

[2] **dementia:** an increasing inability to think clearly

[3] **moss:** a small green or yellow plant that grows on wet soil or rock

[4] **inflammation:** swelling and soreness

[5] **breakdown:** failure

B. Read the text again without pausing. Tell your partner two new pieces of information that you remember.

C. Work as a class or in large groups. Say one thing you remember about the text.

4 | Understanding the Text

A. Answer as many questions as you can without looking at the text. Discuss your answers with a partner.

1. What is the name of the herb that is used to treat Alzheimer's disease?

    a. Chinese moss

    b. Qian Ceng Ta

    c. acetylcholine

2. What country does the herb come from?

    a. China

    b. the United States

    c. Thailand

3. What are the bad effects on the body of this herb?

    a. stomach problems

    b. liver problems

    c. there are no known side effects on the body

4. How has the herb been used in China?

    a. to treat dementia

    b. to make soup

    c. in flower arrangements

5. How many Alzheimer's patients have had their symptoms lessened?

    a. 10

    b. 100,000

    c. all patients with Alzheimer's

B. Check (✔) the correct boxes according to the text. Briefly discuss your answers with a partner.

Type of medication	Treats Alzheimer's disease	Improves brain functioning	Damages the stomach and liver	Does not have negative effects on the body
1. Western medicine	☐	☐	☐	☐
2. Chinese herbal remedy	☐	☐	☐	☐

A **supporting detail** provides evidence, proves, or supports a main idea. Writers use details to develop their arguments. **Supporting details** can be:

facts

opinions

data or statistics

examples

Read ¶**5** on page 101.

The main idea is: The traditional remedy Qian Ceng Ta has been used to treat dementia in China.

The supporting details are:

Doctors there prescribe it to their patients.

Reports from that country suggest that as many as 100,000 Alzheimer's patients have had their symptoms lessened, according to Alan Kozikowski, Ph.D., Georgetown University.

Kozikowski first separated and studied the herbal compound in 1991.

The details all show how and why Qian Ceng Ta has been used to treat dementia in China.

5 | Understanding Supporting Details

Circle the answers that provide supporting details for the main idea, according to the information in the text. Then discuss your answers with a partner.

1. What are the supporting details for ¶**2**?

   a. Alzheimer's is a terrible disease.

   b. Alzheimer's affects 4 million elderly Americans.

   c. Alzheimer's affects 12 million people worldwide.

2. What are the supporting details for ¶**3**?

   a. Qian Ceng Ta comes from a moss.

   b. Qian Ceng Ta is a traditional Chinese remedy.

   c. Qian Ceng Ta is used to treat fever and inflammation.

3. What are the supporting details for ¶**4**?

   a. Alzheimer's sufferers experience memory loss because they get confused.

   b. Alzheimer's sufferers experience memory loss because of acetylcholine breakdown.

   c. Alzheimer's sufferers experience memory loss because they have Alzheimer's.

4. What are the supporting details for ¶5?

   a. Doctor's prescribe Qian Ceng Ta to their patients.

   b. Over 100,000 people's symptoms have been lessened.

   c. An American researcher, Kozikowski, first separated and studied the herbal compound in 1991.

6 | Discussing the Issues

Answer the questions and discuss your answers with a partner.

1. Should the Chinese herb go through a long testing process before being prescribed to patients outside China?

2. What else would you want to know about the herb before seeing it widely used?

3. Have you ever used traditional remedies from your own or other countries? Explain.

Text 2 | Do Herbs Really Work?

1 | Getting Started

A. Check (✔) all the symptoms that you experience when you have a cold.

☐ 1. runny nose   ☐ 4. cough

☐ 2. fever   ☐ 5. extreme tiredness

☐ 3. stomach pain   ☐ 6. sore throat

B. Check (✔) different ways to feel better when you have a cold.

☐ 1. exercise   ☐ 4. drink coffee

☐ 2. rest/sleep   ☐ 5. take medicine

☐ 3. drink tea   ☐ 6. read magazines

2 | Active Previewing

Preview the newspaper article on the next page. Underline the title, the first sentence of each paragraph, and the last sentence of the text as you preview. Then answer the following questions with a partner.

1. What is the topic of the article?

2. What is the main idea of the article?

3 | Reading and Recalling

A. Read the text. Stop after each paragraph and tell a partner two things that you remember about it.

Echinacea: It Works; Oops, It Works Not

BY ELIZABETH WEISE

1   The National Institutes of Health (NIH)[1] has bad news for millions of Americans. They spend $155 million a year on the popular herbal remedy echinacea to treat the cough and runny nose of their common colds. But echinacea, a new study shows, doesn't work.

2   It's not clinically effective[2]," says Ronald Turner. Turner should know. He is an expert on the common cold at the University of Virginia School of Medicine. He wrote the major echinacea study. His study, reported in the current New England Journal of Medicine[3], is the best test ever done on the effectiveness of the herbal remedy, says Stephen Straus. Straus directs the NIH's National Center for Complementary and Alternative Medicine.

3   Turner's is the third study in three years that showed that echinacea was not effective in lessening cold symptoms[4] in children or young adults. The findings of these three studies are the opposite of positive reports on echinacea's effects, mostly from studies done in Europe.

4   In Turner's study, researchers at the University of Virginia randomly gave 399 volunteers either echinacea extract or a placebo[5] for seven days. They then put drops containing cold germs in their noses to give them colds. Finally, the researchers left them alone in hotel rooms so that they couldn't get a cold from anyone or anything else.

5   The goal was to find out if taking echinacea prevents infection or can limit the length of the cold. "The answer was no," Turner says. "It had no effect on the rate at which volunteers got infected or on their symptoms." More than 80% of volunteers in each group got a cold.

6   The problem with colds, which last about seven days, is "no matter what you do, you're going to get better," Straus says. That might make people think that taking echinacea helps when it actually doesn't.

---

[1] **NIH:** part of the U.S. Department of Health and Human Services, it is the main federal agency for supporting and conducting medical research

[2] **not clinically effective:** shown not to be effective when studied in a clinic or hospital

[3] **New England Journal of Medicine:** American journal read by doctors; publishes current medical information

[4] **cold symptoms:** the signs that tell you that you have a cold

[5] **placebo:** a substance given to a patient instead of medicine, without the patient's knowing it is not real

B. Read the text again without pausing. Tell your partner two new pieces of information that you remember.

C. Work as a class or in large groups. Say one thing you remember about the text.

4 | Understanding the Text

Answer as many questions as you can without looking at the text. Discuss your answers with a partner.

1. What is the bad news the NIH has?

   a. Americans spend $155 million on echinacea.

   b. Echinacea, according to a new study, doesn't work.

   c. Cold symptoms include cough and runny nose.

2. Who is Ronald Turner?

   a. author of the American study that shows echinacea doesn't work

   b. author of a European study that shows echinacea to be effective

   c. director of the NIH's National Center for Complementary and Alternative Medicine

3. In order to test whether echinacea works, the Turner study

   a. gave 399 people a placebo.

   b. gave half the volunteers a placebo and the other half echinacea.

   c. gave the volunteers a cold.

 VOCABULARY STRATEGY Understanding Possessive Adjectives

Possessive adjectives are like other adjectives in that they modify nouns or noun phrases. The possessive adjectives are **my, your, her, his, its, our,** and **their**. Sometimes, a possessive adjective refers to a noun or noun phrase in the same sentence, and it is easy to see what the possessive adjective refers to. In other cases, the noun or noun phrase might come before or after the possessive adjective (in another sentence), and it is harder to see.

Read the following sentences.

The National Institutes of Health (NIH) has bad news for millions of Americans. They spend $155 million a year on the popular herbal remedy echinacea to treat the cough and runny nose of *their* common colds. (¶1)

Who has colds? If we refer back to the subject of the second sentence, we can guess that it's *they* who have the colds. Then, we must go back to the first sentence to remember that *they* refers to *Americans*.

5 | Understanding Possessive Adjectives

Circle the possessive adjective in each item and draw an arrow to the noun it refers to. Discuss your answers with a partner.

1. "It's not clinically effective," says Ronald Turner. Turner should know. He is an expert on the common cold at the University of Virginia School of Medicine. He wrote the major echinacea study. His study, reported in the current New England Journal of Medicine, is the best test ever done on the effectiveness of the herbal remedy, says Stephen Straus. (¶2)

2. In Turner's study, researchers at the University of Virginia randomly gave 399 volunteers either echinacea extract or a placebo for seven days. They then put drops containing cold germs in their noses to give them colds. (¶4)

6 | Understanding Supporting Details

A. Check (✔) the reasons that support the claim that echinacea does not work, according to the text. Then briefly discuss your answers with a partner.

☐ 1. Turner believes that echinacea isn't effective in treating colds.

☐ 2. A study was conducted with 399 volunteers.

☐ 3. Half the volunteers were given a placebo and the other half echinacea.

☐ 4. European studies show that echinacea has positive results.

☐ 5. All the volunteers were exposed to cold germs.

☐ 6. The same number of volunteers in each group (80%) got colds.

B. Think about the supporting ideas presented in the text. Are you convinced that echinacea doesn't work? Discuss your answer with a partner.

7 | Discussing the Issues

Answer the questions and discuss your answers with a partner.

1. If one study concludes that a remedy you have been taking does not work, would you still take the remedy? Why or why not?

2. How much should scientific studies influence the decisions people make about how to treat illnesses like the common cold?

3. Would you want to be a volunteer in a medical study? Why or why not?

Text 3 | Food Cures

1 | Getting Started

Look at the photo and then answer the questions. Briefly discuss your answers with a partner.

1. What are your favorite foods?

2. Do you sometimes eat certain foods when you are happy or unhappy?

3. Do some foods have physical effects on you, for example, making you sleepy or excited?

 GRAPHICS Understanding Charts

> **Charts** can show relationships between things in an abbreviated form. To find information, read each column title, then read each row across.

2 | Active Previewing

Preview the chart below and then answer the questions. Discuss your answers with a partner.

1. What are the five categories covered in the chart?

2. How many physical problems does the chart include?

3. Which problem are you most interested in knowing more about?

3 | Scanning

Scan the chart below and then answer the questions. Discuss your answers with a partner.

1. What foods should you avoid if you get migraine headaches?

2. How much quinoa should you eat if you are very tired?

3. What is a good drink to try if you have bad breath?

REMEMBER

Scan, or move your eyes quickly, in order to find the answers.

Food Cures

Problem	Foods to Try	Why/How They Work	How Much to Eat	What to Avoid
Migrane headaches[1]	Fatty fish: trout, sardines, herring, salmon	Omega-3 fatty acids may reduce swelling and pain	One four-to-six ounce serving two or three times a week	Processed meats, MSG, red wine, chocolate, hard cheeses
Extreme tiredness	Quinoa, a whole grain	Three major nutrients that give you energy: protein, B vitamins, and iron	Eat one-and-a half cups of cooked quinoa daily	High-sugar foods and caffeine
Stress	Low-fat popcorn, honey, graham crackers, whole-wheat pretzels	Low-fat carbohydrates increase the production of serotonin[2] in the brain	A bowl of cereal or a slice of toast, a cup of popcorn	Caffeine
Heartburn[3]	Ginger	May help strengthen the valve between your stomach and throat	Add one-half to one teaspoon fresh ginger to a cup of hot water	High-fat foods, spicy foods, acidic foods
Gas	Peppermint tea, fennel seeds	Both help relax bowel muscles[4]	Drink one cup of peppermint tea or eat a half teaspoon fennel seeds after a meal	Sodas; beans, tofu, and some vegetables
Bad breath	Tea–black, green or oolong	Tea stops the spread of bacteria in the mouth	One cup after a meal	Onions, garlic, cabbage

---

[1] **migraine headaches:** severe and recurring pain in the head

[2] **serotonin:** neurotransmitter responsible for mood

[3] **heartburn:** an unpleasant feeling in your stomach or chest

[4] **bowel muscles:** the muscles that are involved in digesting food

4 | Discussing the Issues

Answer the questions and discuss your answers with a partner.

1. Which of the food cures do you think you will try?

2. Which of the foods to be avoided would you have a hard time giving up?

3. Do you have a family member or friend who might find information from this chart useful? If so, who and why?

Text 4 | Caffeine

1 | Getting Started

A. Match each photo to the best description. Discuss your answers with a partner.

_____ 1. A traditional cafe in the Middle East

_____ 2. A tea ceremony in Japan

_____ 3. Scene from an American coffee shop

_____ 4. Teenagers taking a soda break

B. Check (✔) what the four photos have in common. Briefly discuss your answers with a partner.

☐ a. All the photos were taken in the same country.

☐ b. All the photos show old people.

☐ c. All the photos show men.

☐ d. All the photos show people socializing and drinking something.

☐ e. All the drinks shown have caffeine in them.

2 | Active Previewing

Preview the online article on the next page. Underline the title, the first sentence of each paragraph, and the last sentence of the text. Then write *T* for *True* or *F* for *False* according to the text. Discuss your answers with a partner.

_____ **1.** Caffeine is not a drug.

_____ **2.** People around the world consume 120,000 tons of caffeine every year.

_____ **3.** Caffeine is found in chocolate.

_____ **4.** Moderate amounts of caffeine make people think quickly and clearly.

3 | Reading and Recalling

A. Read the text. Stop after each paragraph and tell a partner two things that you remember about it.

Caffeine

1 It's 11:00 P.M. and you've already had a full day of work or school. You're tired and you know you could use some sleep. But you still haven't finished everything you need to do or watched the movie that's due back tomorrow. So instead of going to bed, you reach for the remote—and the caffeine.

2 **What Is Caffeine?**
Caffeine is a drug that is naturally produced in the leaves and seeds of many plants. It's also produced artificially and added to certain foods. Caffeine is part of the same group of drugs sometimes used to treat asthma[1].

3 It is estimated that around the world people consume 120,000 tons[2] of caffeine annually[3]. Look at it another way. Every one of the 5 million people on the earth drinks one beverage—one cup—containing caffeine a day. Tea is the caffeinated beverage of choice.

4 Caffeine is defined as a drug because it stimulates[4] the central nervous system, the brain and spinal cord. Caffeine causes the heart to beat faster and makes a person feel wide awake. Most people who are sensitive to caffeine experience a temporary increase in energy. And they feel happier.

continued

---
[1] **asthma:** an illness that causes difficulty in breathing
[2] **ton:** a unit of measuring weight equal to 2240 pounds
[3] **annually:** every year
[4] **stimulates:** makes a part of the body active

continued

5   Caffeine is in tea leaves, coffee beans, chocolate, many soft drinks, and pain relievers. In its natural form, caffeine tastes very bitter. This is why most caffeinated drinks go through processing to hide the bitter taste.

6   **Got the Jitters?**
The amount of caffeine in different beverages varies greatly. Many sodas have added caffeine. A 12-ounce cola can have between 38 mg and 71.2 milligrams (mg) of caffeine. A 5-ounce cup of brewed coffee, on average, contains 115 mg of caffeine. Iced tea (12 ounces) contains 70 mg. Dark chocolate has approximately 20 mg per ounce. Milk chocolate contains much less: 6 mg.

7   If people take it in moderate amounts (a single can of soda or cup of coffee), caffeine increases their ability to think quickly and clearly. Higher doses of caffeine (several cups of coffee) can cause anxiety, dizziness, headaches, and the jitters. Caffeine can make it difficult to sleep.

8   Caffeine is addictive and may cause withdrawal symptoms[5] for those who suddenly stop consuming it. These include severe headaches, muscle aches, temporary depression, and irritability.

9   Caffeine moves through the body within a few hours after it's consumed and then passes through the urine. It's not stored in the body, but you may feel its effects for up to six hours if you're sensitive to it.

10 **Moderation Is the Key**
Effects of caffeine vary from one person to the next. However, doctors recommend that people should consume no more than about 100 milligrams of caffeine daily. That might sound like a lot, but one espresso contains about 100 milligrams of caffeine!

---

[5] **withdrawal symptoms:** the painful or unpleasant effects of giving up a drug you are dependant on

B. Read the text again without pausing. Tell your partner two new pieces of information that you remember.

C. Work as a class or in large groups. Say one thing you remember about the text.

5 | Understanding the Text

A. Answer as many questions as you can without looking at the text. There may be more than one answer. Discuss your answers with a partner.

1. What is caffeine?

   a. coffee

   b. a naturally occurring drug found in the leaves and seeds of plants

   c. an artificially produced drug added to certain foods and drinks

2. How much caffeine is consumed in one day around the world?

   a. very little

   b. more than 100,00 tons

   c. about 5 million caffeinated beverages

3. You can find caffeine in

   a. coffee and tea

   b. chocolate

   c. some soft drinks

4. What are the effects of caffeine?

   a. In moderate doses, caffeine makes people think more quickly and clearly.

   b. In high doses, caffeine makes people think more quickly and clearly.

   c. Caffeine has no effect on most people.

5. What happens to you if you regularly drink beverages with caffeine, and then stop?

   a. You may experience withdrawal symptoms.

   b. You may get headaches and muscle aches.

   c. You may be in a bad mood.

6. Doctors recommend that people should consume no more than about _____ of caffeine daily.

   a. 10 milligrams

   b. 100 milligrams

   c. 1000 milligrams

B. Complete the chart by scanning for information in the text. Discuss your answers with a partner.

Food or beverage	Amount of caffeine
1. Dark chocolate	
2.	6 mg. per ounce
3. 5 oz. brewed coffee	
4. 12 oz. cola	
5.	70 mg.

6 | Understanding Apposition

Write the words in apposition according to the text. Discuss your answers with a partner.

1. one beverage (¶3) _____

2. the central nervous system (¶4) _____

3. moderate amounts (¶7) _____

4. higher doses (¶7) _____

REMEMBER

A word or phrase that means the same as a noun and is next to that noun in the sentence is said to be in apposition to the noun.
See page 89 for more on *apposition*.

7 | Understanding Vocabulary in Context—Definitions

A. Read the following sentences from *Text 1*. Check (✔) the part of speech for each underlined word. Then write its definition on the line.

1. It's also produced <u>artificially</u> and added to certain foods.

   ☐ a. noun   ☐ b. adverb   ☐ c. adjective

   _____

2. This is why most caffeinated drinks go through processing to hide their <u>bitter</u> taste.

   ☐ a. noun   ☐ b. adverb   ☐ c. adjective

   _____

3. If people take it in <u>moderate</u> amounts (a single can of soda or cup of coffee), caffeine increases their ability to think quickly and clearly.

   ☐ a. noun   ☐ b. adverb   ☐ c. adjective

   _____

B. With a partner, try to define the following words. Then use the footnotes from the text to check your answers.

1. asthma _____

2. ton _____

3. annually _____

4. stimulates _____

5. withdrawal symptoms _____

8 | Understanding Supporting Details

Answer the following questions. Discuss your answers with a partner.

1. What are two or three supporting details for the first section of the text: "What Is Caffeine?"?

   _____

   _____

   _____

   _____

2. What are two or three supporting details for the second section of the text: "Got the Jitters?"?

   _____

   _____

   _____

   _____

3. What are two or three supporting details for the last section of the text: "Moderation Is the Key"?

   _____

   _____

   _____

   _____

9 | Discussing the Issues

Answer the questions and discuss your answers with a partner.

1. Do you know of any rituals related to caffeine in other cultures?

2. Is caffeine bad or good for you?

3. If you consume caffeine, is there anything you would change about your habits after reading this article?

Putting It On Paper

A. Write a paragraph on one of these topics.

1. Should we look around the world for herbal cures for illnesses, even if they are not always found to be effective? Explain your ideas and give examples.

2. Can foods change your moods? Give specific examples to illustrate your opinion.

Steps for your paragraph

a. Write your opinion or main idea in the first sentence; this is your topic sentence.

b. Write three sentences with details—facts, data, examples, etc.—that prove your opinion or support the main idea.

c. Summarize your ideas in a final sentence.

B. Exchange paragraphs with a partner. Read your partner's paragraph and answer the questions in the checklist. Give feedback to your partner.

✔ CHECKLIST
1. Can you identify the main idea or your partner's opinion about the topic?
2. Are there three examples to support the topic? Number them on the paper.
3. Are you persuaded by your partner's examples or reasons? Explain below.
4. Is any of the information not related to the topic? If yes, please underline it on your partner's paper and then write it below.

_____

_____

_____

_____

_____

_____

C. Revise your work based on your partner's feedback.

Taking It Online | Researching Foods

A. With a partner, use the Internet to research foods that heal or cure.

1. Use Google (www.google.com) or another major search engine to find sites with the information you want. What words do you think you should type in the search box to begin your search? Write them here.

_____

_____

2. Preview the sites as you would a magazine article or an essay. Scan for information about three different food cures or remedies from three different countries.

B. Complete the table below with the information you find.

Type of food	Country of origin	Benefits	Problems
1.			
2.			
3.			

C. Following up. Tell your classmates about one of the food cures you discovered.

Experimental Science

Answer the questions and briefly discuss your answers with a partner.

1. Do you know a lot about science?

2. Look at the photos. Which area of scientific study do you think each represents?

3. What are some areas of science that you are interested in?

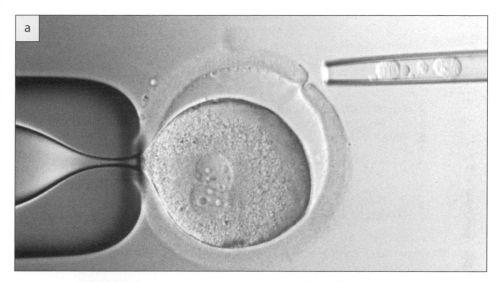

a

b

c

Text 1 | The Work of One Scientist

1 | Getting Started

A. Answer the questions and briefly discuss your answers with a partner.

1. Have you ever climbed a tree? If you have, how high off the ground did you climb? If you haven't, why not?

2. What/who lives in and around trees?

3. What else, besides providing shelter for living things, are trees good for?

4. What do you think would interest a scientist about trees?

B. Check (✔) all the statements that reflect your opinion. Discuss your answers with a partner.

☐ 1. Scientists are dreamers.

☐ 2. Scientists are problem-solvers.

☐ 3. Scientists work alone in laboratories.

☐ 4. Scientists collaborate with others.

☐ 5. Scientists are teachers.

☐ 6. Scientists guard their research carefully.

2 | Active Previewing

Preview the academic text on the next page. Underline the title, the first sentence of each paragraph, and the last sentence of the text. Then answer the following questions with a partner.

1. What do you think the text is about?

2. How is the title "Highways to Heaven" related to the last sentence of the last paragraph?

3 | Reading and Recalling

A. Read the text. Stop after each paragraph and tell a partner two things that you remember about it.

Highways to Heaven

by Margaret Lowman

1   As children, we learn to love trees. We climb them, we build forts in their boughs[1], we lie on the grass beneath them and watch their branches sway in the wind, we envy monkeys and birds their agility, and we find fascination with the tiny beasts that inhabit decaying tree trunks. Perhaps strangest, we spend most of our time gazing upward, attempting to sort out the complex array of branches and foliage[2] that is difficult to observe. We wonder what sorts of creatures inhabit those lofty crevices beyond our reach.

2   When I returned from Australia to my position as a biology professor at Williams College, I wanted to share the wonders of the forest canopy[3] with my enthusiastic biology students. During my tenure as a professor of undergraduates, single-rope techniques for access into the forest canopy began to frustrate me. I could not share the canopy with my students by using ropes, for only one person at a time could mount[4] them.

3   Then, like a gift from heaven, a letter came to me one day from an arborist[5] in nearby Amherst. He not only had expertise in construction and working in treetops, but he also had strong convictions about the conservation[6] of tropical forests. Would I consider collaborating? Bart Bouricius and I brainstormed for several months about the design of our temperate-canopy walkway in Hopkins Forest. Later, we received a small grant from a local foundation interested in environmental concerns. Our budget was a modest $2,500, which provided two platforms[7] connected by one bridge with a 75-foot access ladder, plus safety equipment for the students.

Finally, with a price tag less than that of most microscopes, the walkway proved an excellent investment for the advancement of science.

4   The walkway concept became very popular as a teaching and research tool throughout North America. We expanded to tropical rain forests, with projects, for example, in Belize, Borneo, Ecuador, and others pending in Costa Rica and Mexico. Our network of walkways grows every year. Comparative studies are now possible in places like Australia, Samoa, North America, Central America, and South America. Even Africa boasts a walkway site in Uganda, although I have not yet been fortunate enough to visit it. I hope that over the next decade students can initiate additional comparative studies of canopy biology. The platforms and walkways will provide them with a relatively simple and safe method of canopy access.

---

[1] **boughs:** the limbs or branches of trees

[2] **foliage:** the leaves of trees

[3] **canopy:** the top leaves and branches of trees that sometimes grow together

[4] **mount:** climb

[5] **arborist:** someone who specializes in trees

[6] **conservation:** the protection of natural things such as animals, plants, or forests to prevent them from being destroyed

[7] **platforms:** tall or high structures built so that people can work from them

B. Read the text again without pausing. Tell your partner two new pieces of information that you remember.

C. Work as a class or in large groups. Say one thing you remember about the text.

4 | Understanding the Text

A. Complete as many statements as you can without looking at the text. Discuss your answers with a partner.

1. Margaret Lowman is

    a. a scientist who studies dolphins.

    b. a scientist who studies living things in tree canopies.

    c. a road builder.

2. Lowman was frustrated with single-rope techniques for canopy access because

    a. her students got tangled in the ropes.

    b. she wanted to built forts in the trees.

    c. only one person at a time could climb into the canopy and work there.

3. Lowman, with the help of arborist Bart Bouricius, designed and built

    a. ladders and platform and bridges to access the canopy for scientific study.

    b. a highway to the sky.

    c. a tree house for her kids to play in.

B. Complete the chart according to the text. Then discuss your answers with a partner.

Problems	Solutions
1. The height of trees	*Single-rope technique to climb to the tops of trees*
2. What she wanted to study lives in the canopy	
3. The single-rope technique allows only one person at a time to work	
4. A limited budget	
5. Expanding her research beyond rain forests	

5 | Understanding Possessive Adjectives

Complete the chart with all the possessive adjectives from *Text 1*. Then write the noun or noun phrase each adjective refers to. Discuss your answers with a partner.

Paragraph	Possessive adjective	Noun/noun phrase it refers to
¶1	their, their,	trees, monkeys and birds,
¶2		
¶3		
¶4		

 READING SKILL Detecting Sequence with Sequence Markers

Recognizing and understanding sequence markers helps you understand sequence, or the order in which something occurred or was done. Texts can become confusing when you cannot follow the sequence the author is writing about.

Typical sequence markers include specific time expressions like dates and expressions of relative time like *first, second, last* or *first, then, next.*

Read the following sentences.

1. During my tenure as a professor of undergraduates, single-rope techniques for access into the forest canopy began to frustrate me. I could not share the canopy with my students by using ropes, for only one person at a time could mount them. (¶2)

2. Then, like a gift from heaven, a letter came to me one day from an arborist in nearby Amherst. (¶3)

While the first example does not include a sequence marker, in the second sentence, the word *then* is a signal to the reader that events are being recounted in chronological order. First, Professor Lowman gets frustrated that only one person at a time can climb into the canopy. Second, she receives a letter that leads to a solution to this problem.

6 | Detecting Sequence with Sequence Markers

Answer the following question. Then discuss your answer with a partner.

What are the sequences in Lowman's story?

_____

_____

_____

 VOCABULARY STRATEGY Understanding Vocabulary in Context—Examples

Examples often explain unfamiliar words in a text, give specific facts to expand a generalization, or tell stories to illuminate an idea. Examples are frequently given with phrases like *for example, such as,* and *like,* or sometimes they follow a colon (:).

Read the following sentence.

We expanded to tropical rain forests, with *projects,* for example, in Belize, Borneo, Ecuador, and others pending in Costa Rica and Mexico. (¶4)

We can infer that *expanded* means to grow. The phrase *for example* indicates that *Belize, Borneo, Ecuador, and others pending in Costa Rica and Mexico* are where the projects are located. We also learn that there are tropical rain forests in Belize, Borneo, Ecuador, Costa Rica, and Mexico.

7 | Understanding Vocabulary in Context—Examples

Answer the following question. Discuss your answer with a partner.

Where are comparative studies possible now? (¶4)

_____

_____

8 | Discussing the Issues

1. How did Margaret Lowman's work advance science?

2. What are some potential benefits of Margaret Lowman's work studying the rain forest canopy?

3. Tourists can also now climb into the rain forest canopy. Would you be interested in doing this? Why or why not?

Text 2 | Accidental Discovery

1 | Getting Started

A. Answer the questions and briefly discuss your answers with a partner.

1. Have you ever been sick enough to take an antibiotic like penicillin?

2. Do you know of any cases when a person got sicker because he or she didn't get the necessary medicine?

3. If you had the ability (either through science or magic), which diseases would you invent cures for?

B. Check (✔) whether you agree or disagree. Briefly discuss your answers with a partner.

Statements	Agree	Disagree
1. Scientific discoveries are always made calmly and carefully, in clean environments.	☐	☐
2. Scientists often do not find what they are looking for.	☐	☐
3. Penicillin, and similar antibiotics, have been around forever, curing sick patients.	☐	☐
4. Scientists spend all their time in laboratories, cut off from the problems of the real world.	☐	☐

2 | Scanning

Scan the text on the next page for the two quotations from Alexander Fleming. Then answer the following question.

What do the quotations tell you about Fleming and his discovery?

> **REMEMBER**
>
> Have a goal in mind when you scan. In this case, look for quotation marks.
> See page 37 for more on *scanning a text*.

3 | Active Previewing

Preview the magazine article on the next page . Underline the title, the first sentence of each paragraph, and the last sentence of the text. Then answer the following questions with a partner.

What do you think the text is about?

4 | Reading and Recalling

A. Read the text. Stop after each paragraph and tell a partner two things that you remember about it.

Alexander Fleming: Discoverer of "Miracle Drug" Penicillin

BY IAN LUNDY

1   In his cluttered[1] research laboratory[2], bacteriologist Alexander Fleming made an accidental discovery that would forever change the world of modern medicine.

2   He was clearing his sink of a pile of petri dishes, in which he had been growing bacteria[3], and was checking each one before discarding it. Then the contents of one dish caught his eye. Common fungal mold, like that found on stale bread, had grown and appeared to be killing off the harmful bacteria inside. Next, Fleming conducted a series of tests on the fungus, *penicillium notatum,* and successfully isolated the antibiotic[4] substance which he called penicillin.

3   "One sometimes finds what one is not looking for," remarked Fleming in typically understated fashion.

4   What the Scottish scientist had found in September 1928 proved to be the greatest breakthrough[5] in the treatment of infection[6] the world had witnessed. At first it was underestimated by the medical community. Later, Fleming's work was taken on in the 1930s by chemists Howard Florey and Ernst Chain. They purified penicillin to a more useful treatment form. With their work, the scale of Fleming's discovery became obvious.

5   British and American drug companies mass-produced penicillin. The new drug was hailed as a medical miracle during World War II when it saved millions of lives by crippling the biggest wartime killer—medical wounds.

> [Fleming's] exposure to the terrible battlefield wounds that claimed the lives of thousands of soldiers strengthened his determination to develop a powerful and useful antiseptic.

6   During World War I, Fleming served as a captain in the Royal Army Medical Corps, working in the laboratory of a battlefield hospital in France. His exposure to the terrible battlefield wounds that claimed the lives of thousands of soldiers strengthened his determination to develop a powerful and useful antiseptic.

7   In the early 1920s, again by accident, he had discovered lysozyme, now known in medical circles as "the little brother of penicillin." An enzyme occurring in bodily fluids, for example, in tears, lysozyme has a natural antibacterial affect. First, Fleming had sneezed into a bacteria-laced petri dish. Several days later, he noticed that the bacteria had been destroyed by the mucus. But lysozyme was not effective against the stronger infectious agents and Fleming kept searching until his monumental discovery several years later.

8   "Nature makes penicillin, I just found it," he said at the time. Penicillin is today used commonly along with many other antibiotics, for example, amoxicillin or tetracycline, to treat all kinds of bacteria, prevent infection, and save lives.

---

[1] **cluttered:** filled with too many things, messy

[2] **laboratory:** special room where a scientist tests and prepares his or her work

[3] **bacteria:** very small living things that cause disease

[4] **antibiotic:** a substance that kills bacteria and prevents infections

[5] **breakthrough:** an important new discovery

[6] **infection:** disease caused by bacteria

B. Read the text again without pausing. Tell your partner two new pieces of information that you remember.

C. Work as a class or in large groups. Say one thing you remember about the text.

5 | Understanding the Text

A. Complete as many statements as you can without referring to the text. Discuss your answers with a partner.

1. Alexander Fleming's discovery of penicillin

    a. made very little difference in the world.

    b. had a huge effect on modern medicine.

    c. affected only soldiers.

2. Fleming did not throw away the petri dish with mold in it because the mold was

    a. something he wanted to eat for dinner.

    b. cleaning the dish.

    c. killing off harmful bacteria.

3. Before he discovered penicillin, Fleming

    a. worked as a soldier.

    b. discovered lysozyme, "the little brother of penicillin."

    c. was not interested in science.

B. Check (✔) whether the following are topics or main ideas in the text. Briefly discuss your answers with a partner.

Topics or main ideas	Yes	Not found in the text
1. the discovery of penicillin	☐	☐
2. Alexander Fleming made a minor discovery when he discovered penicillin.	☐	☐
3. Alexander Fleming, with his discovery of penicillin, changed the course of modern medicine.	☐	☐
4. chicken eggs	☐	☐

6 | Detecting Sequence with Sequence Markers

A. Put the following sequence markers into the correct time order, 1 to 4.

WWII	1928	WWI	the early 1920s

1. _____

2. _____

3. _____

4. _____

B. Add the following discoveries to the correct time periods in your answers to part *A*.

   lysozyme   penicillin

C. Complete the following sentences according to the text. Discuss your answers with a partner.

1. First, (¶7) _____

2. Several days later, (¶7) _____

3. Several years later, (¶7) _____

7 | Understanding Vocabulary in Context—Examples

In each sentence, underline the example and draw an arrow to the word or words the example illustrates. Discuss your answers with a partner.

1. An enzyme occurring in bodily fluids, for example, in tears, lysozyme has a natural antibacterial effect. (¶7)

2. Penicillin is today used commonly along with many other antibiotics, for example, amoxicillin or tetracycline, to treat all kinds of bacteria, prevent infection, and save lives. (¶8)

8 | Discussing the Issues

Answer the questions and discuss your answers with a partner.

1. Do you think the discovery of penicillin was inevitable? In other words, do you think someone else would have discovered penicillin if Fleming had not?

2. How has Fleming's discovery changed the world? Can you think of any examples?

3. Many scientists have discovered things by accident. How do you explain this?

Text 3 | How Much Sleep Do We Need?

1 | Getting Started

Look at the photo and then answer the questions. Briefly discuss your answers with a partner.

1. How much sleep do you get every night?

2. Do you ever worry that you aren't getting enough sleep? How much sleep do you feel would be the perfect amount for you?

3. Why do we need sleep?

2 | Active Previewing

Preview the bar graph on the next page and then answer the questions. Discuss your answers with a partner.

1. What is the title of the bar graph? How is the title related to the information in the graph?

2. What do you notice about the size of the animals in the graph, looking from left to right?

3. What do you notice about the number of hours of sleep, looking from left to right?

> **REMEMBER**
>
> Look for statistical information in bar graphs. Information is presented visually in vertical and horizontal directions. See page 45 for more on *understanding bar graphs*.

Counting Sleep

Body size appears to be one of the main things that determines the amount of sleep that a species needs. In general, the larger the animal, the less sleep it requires. Data suggest that one of the functions[1] of sleep is to repair damage to brain cells. The higher metabolic rates[2] of small animals lead to increased cellular injury and may, consequently, require more time for repair.

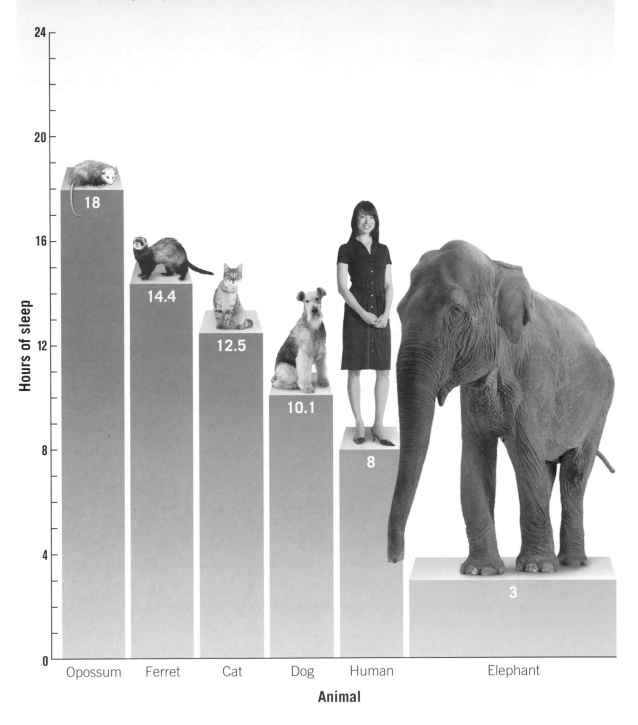

Hours of sleep

Opossum	Ferret	Cat	Dog	Human	Elephant
18	14.4	12.5	10.1	8	3

Animal

---

[1] **functions:** normal activities; purposes

[2] **metabolic rates:** speed at which growth processes occur

3 | Scanning

Scan the bar graph for answers to the following questions. Discuss your answers with a partner.

1. Which animal sleeps the most? How many hours? _____

2. Which animal sleeps the least? How many hours? _____

3. How many hours of sleep do humans need? _____

4 | Discussing the Issues

Answer the questions and discuss your answers with a partner.

1. How is the size of an animal's body related to the amount of sleep it needs?

2. Based on what you learned from the graph, how much sleep do you predict a mouse needs?

3. Are you surprised by how humans compare with other animals in their sleep needs? If you are, what did you think before you studied the graph?

Text 4 | Stomach Trouble Cured

1 | Getting Started

Match the term with the best definition. Briefly discuss your answers with a partner.

_____ 1. Australia

a. a serious wound in the stomach that causes pain and internal bleeding

_____ 2. stomach ulcer

b. a very small living thing that causes disease

_____ 3. the Nobel Prize

c. the English-speaking country on an island continent in the Southern Hemisphere

_____ 4. bacterium

d. a prize given for outstanding research in a specific field, for example, literature or medicine

Skimming is moving your eyes over a text as you read quickly. You skim when you want to get a general idea about the information in the text but do not need to know all of the details.

Skimming is a good way to preview a text. It also helps you save time. For example, you skim when you want to see if the full text is something you want to read or if it will have the information you need. To skim:

1. Read the title and any subtitles.

2. Read one or two paragraphs at the beginning.

3. Read the first and/or last sentence of the other paragraphs.

4. Look quickly at the other paragraphs. Read only a few words here and there. Notice names, places, dates and numbers, and words in bold or italic print.

5. Read the last paragraph.

2 | Skimming

Skim the article in three minutes or less. Discuss your answers with a partner.

1. How old is Dr. J. Robin Warren? Dr. Barry J. Marshall?

_____

2. In what year did the two researchers win the Nobel Prize in Medicine?

_____

3. How much money did they receive?

_____

4. What percentage of lower stomach ulcers are caused by Helicobacter pylori?

_____

5. In what year did the research get its start?

_____

3 | Active Previewing

Preview the academic text on the next page. Underline the title, the first sentence of each paragraph, and the last sentence of the text. Then answer the following questions with a partner.

1. What is the text about?

2. Which sentence that you underlined states the main point of the article?

A. Read the text. Stop after each paragraph and tell a partner two things that you remember about it.

They Found Their Nobel Inside Their Stomachs

by Thomas H. Maugh

1   Two Australian researchers discovered that a bacterium[1], not stress or spicy[2] food, causes stomach ulcers. They were given the 2005 Nobel Prize in Medicine, a $1.3 million award, for this important discovery.

2   Dr. J. Robin Warren, 68, and Dr. Barry J. Marshall, 54, changed opinions that doctors held for decades. They found a bacterium called Helicobacter pylori and demonstrated that it could produce stomach ulcers, serious wounds in the stomach. The researchers "produced one of the most radical and important changes in the last 50 years in the perception of a medical condition," said Lord Robert May, president of the Royal Society.

3   The slow acceptance of their idea began when Marshall swallowed a bottle of Helicobacter pylori. He wanted to show that the bacterium caused stomach illness. It did. He got very sick. Researchers now know that Helicobacter pylori causes more than 90 percent of lower stomach ulcers and 80 percent of upper intestinal ulcers, the Nobel committee said.

continued

---

[1] **bacterium:** very small living things that can cause disease

[2] **spicy:** food with a strong taste that might give you a burning feeling in your mouth

continued

4   In the years before their research was accepted, many fellow scientists did not believe them. Drug companies that made money selling medicine for controlling the symptoms of ulcers didn't believe them either. Finally, doctors began to widely accept the discovery when they observed the results in their patients. Ulcers could be cured quickly with a short course of antibiotics[3]. "I was treating my patients[4] with the then-traditional methods for ulcers when his work was first published. I truly did not believe it until I saw what it did for my patients," said Dr. David Peura of the University of Virginia.

5   The research got its start in 1979. Warren, a pathologist[5], observed what he thought was a bacterium in the lower part of the stomach in more than half his patients. He also saw areas of swelling around the bacteria. He was surprised by the discovery because doctors had argued for decades that the inside of the stomach was too sour for any bacteria to grow. Researchers now know that the bacterium infects about half the population around the world. Only a small number of those infected develop ulcers. The discovery that ulcers were caused by a bacterium led to research on other diseases that might have an infectious origin, the Nobel committee said.

---

[3] **antibiotics:** drugs that are used to kill bacteria and cure infections
[4] **patients:** people being take care of by doctors
[5] **pathologist:** someone who studies the causes and effects of illnesses

B. Read the text again without pausing. Tell your partner two new pieces of information that you remember.

C. Work as a class or in large groups. Say one thing you remember about the text.

5 | Understanding the Text

A. Complete as many statements as you can without looking at the text. Discuss your answers with a partner.

1. Two Australian researchers discovered the cause of stomach ulcers is

   a. spicy food.

   b. a bacterium.

   c. stress.

2. Because of their important discovery, they won

   a. the Nobel Prize in Literature.

   b. the Nobel Prize in Medicine.

   c. the Australian Prize for Ulcers.

3. In order to convince people that the bacterium was truly the cause of ulcers, Marshall

   a. argued with them.

   b. wrote letters to doctors and drug companies explaining his views.

   c. proved his claim by swallowing the bacterium himself and getting sick.

B. Write *T* for *True* and *F* for *False* according to the text. Discuss your answers with a partner.

_____ **1.** Dr. J. Robin Warren and Dr. Barry J. Marshall changed opinions that doctors held for decades about what causes stomach ulcers.

_____ **2.** They had to convince doctors but not drug companies.

_____ **3.** Doctors who treated their patients with antibiotics and saw them get healthy still didn't believe the researchers.

_____ **4.** In 1979, Dr. Warren was surprised to discover a bacterium and swelling in the stomach of many of his patients.

_____ **5.** Researchers now know that the bacterium infects only a small percentage of the world's population.

_____ **6.** The Nobel committee said that this discovery led to other important discoveries.

6 | Understanding Supporting Details

Write two supporting details for each main idea. Discuss your answers with a partner.

1. Dr. J. Robin Warren, 68, and Dr. Barry J. Marshall, 54, changed opinions that doctors held for decades. (¶2)

a. _____

_____

b. _____

_____

2. The slow acceptance of their idea began when Marshall swallowed a bottle of Helicobacter pylori. (¶3)

a. _____

_____

b. _____

_____

3. Finally, doctors began to widely accept the discovery when they observed the results in their patients. (¶4)

a. _____

_____

b. _____

_____

7 | Detecting Sequence with Sequence Markers

Read the following sentences from the text and put them in chronological order from 1 to 6. Use the sequence markers to help you. Discuss your answers with a partner.

a. _____ The slow acceptance of their idea began when Marshall swallowed a bottle of Helicobacter pylori.

b. _____ The research got its start in 1979.

c. _____ They were given the 2005 Nobel Prize in Medicine, a $1.3 million award, for this important discovery.

d. _____ In the years before their research was accepted, many fellow scientists did not believe them.

e. _____ Researchers now know that Helicobacter pylori causes more than 90 percent of lower stomach ulcers and 80 percent of upper intestinal ulcers, the Nobel committee said.

f. _____ Finally, doctors began to widely accept the discovery when they observed the results in their patients.

8 | Discussing the Issues

Answer the questions and discuss your answers with a partner.

1. Do you think it's common that scientists face disbelief when they discover new medicines or causes for diseases? Why or why not?

2. In your view, should scientists be awarded large sums of money for making important discoveries?

3. What do you think Drs. Warren and Marshall will do with the money they won?

Putting It On Paper

A. Write a paragraph on one of these topics.

1. What scientific discovery have you most benefited from and why?

2. Are scientists valued in your society or country?

3. Is science a creative field?

Steps for your paragraph

    a. Write your opinion or main idea in the first sentence; this is your topic sentence.

    b. Write three sentences with details—facts, data, examples, etc.—that prove your opinion or support the main idea.

    c. Summarize your ideas in a final sentence.

B. Exchange paragraphs with a partner. Read your partner's paragraph and answer the questions in the checklist. Give feedback to your partner.

✔ CHECKLIST
1. Can you identify the main idea or your partner's opinion about the topic?
2. Are there three examples to support the topic? Number them on the paper.
3. Are you persuaded by your partner's examples or reasons? Explain below.
4. Is any of the information not related to the topic? If yes, please underline it on your partner's paper and then write it below.

_____

_____

_____

_____

_____

_____

_____

C. Revise your work based on your partner's feedback.

Taking It Online | Famous Scientists

A. With a partner, use the Internet to research a famous scientist.

1. Together, decide on a scientist you want to learn more about.

2. Use Google (www.google.com) or another major search engine to find sites with the information you want. An encyclopedia Website like Encyclopaedia Britannica Online (www.britannica.com) might also be useful.

3. Preview the sites as you would a magazine article or an essay.

ONLINE TIP

If you can't think of a scientist, try typing in the key words **famous scientists** in the search box of your search engine.

B. Complete the chart below with the information you find.

Information about _____
your scientist
Year of birth:
Year of death:
Nationality:
Area of scientific study:
Famous discoveries:

C. Following up. Share with your classmates what you learned about the scientist.

Chapter 8

Secretive Behavior

Answer the questions and briefly discuss your answers with a partner.

1. Do you keep secrets?

2. Look at the photos. What do you imagine the people in the photos are revealing?

3. Do you think keeping secrets is good or bad, and why?

Text 1 | Secret Salary

1 | Getting Started

A. Answer only the questions you feel comfortable answering. Briefly discuss your answers with a partner. Tell why you felt comfortable answering some questions but not others.

1. How old are you?

2. How much do you weigh?

3. How much money did you earn last year?

B. Check (✔) all the reasons why people might not say how much money they earn.

☐ 1. They make a big salary.

☐ 2. They make a low salary.

☐ 3. They feel they earn more than they should.

☐ 4. They feel they earn less than they should.

☐ 5. They earn much more than other people in the same type of position.

☐ 6. They earn much less than other people in the same type of position.

2 | Active Previewing

Preview the newspaper article on the next page. Underline the title, the first sentence of each paragraph, and the last sentence of the text as you preview. Then answer the following questions with a partner.

1. **Who** is the article about?

2. **What** has the person been able to do for a long time?

3. **Where** does the person work?

3 | Reading and Recalling

A. Read the text. Stop after each paragraph and tell a partner two things that you remember about it.

Penn State's Long-Held Secret: The President's Salary

BY PAUL FAIN

1   Graham B. Spanier, president of the Pennsylvania State University system, is different from other public-college presidents. He has been able to keep his salary a secret for a long time.

2   As a "state-related" institution, Penn State has refused to tell Mr. Spanier's salary. Stephen J. MacCarthy, Penn State's vice president for university relations, explains why. He says the university's Board of Trustees[1] believes that telling employee salaries is "bad business practice." It could cause morale problems. It could make it easier to recruit from the university's ranks. "It's just been a board policy[2] that salaries ought to be a private matter," says Mr. MacCarthy.

3   Now, for the first time, Penn State officials have released[3] President Spanier's salary to the *Chronicle of Higher Education*. Every year, the *Chronicle* does a survey[4] to find out top executives'[5] salaries. This is what the *Chronicle* found out. Mr. Spanier will be paid $492,000 by the university in 2005–6. In addition, he lives in a university-owned home. He drives a car provided by the university. Mr. Spanier's total compensation[6] ranks 25th among presidents of 139 public universities surveyed by the *Chronicle*.

4   The *Chronicle* asked why Penn State decided to release Mr. Spanier's compensation. Mr. MacCarthy responded that the president "felt it was an important thing to do." He said Mr. Spanier spoke with the board after receiving the *Chronicle's* request. Both agreed to release the information.

5   People at Penn State and news outlets in Pennsylvania have long debated the secrecy surrounding Mr. Spanier's salary. The salary was made public only twice before—in 1995, when Mr. Spanier was hired, and in 1999, when it was included on an Internal Revenue Service (IRS) form.

---

[1] **Board of Trustees:** a group of people who make decisions about university rules and policies

[2] **policy:** a decision about a certain action or direction

[3] **released:** made public

[4] **survey:** a set of questions you ask a large number of people to find out their opinions or behavior

[5] **top executives:** people who have important, high-level jobs

[6] **total compensation:** total salary package, including money and other things like a home or a car

B. Read the text again without pausing. Tell your partner two new pieces of information that you remember.

C. Work as a class or in large groups. Say one thing you remember about the text.

4 | Understanding the Text

A. Answer as many questions as you can without looking at the text. Discuss your answers with a partner.

1. What is the secret President Spanier has been able to keep for a long time?

   a. his weight

   b. his marital status

   c. his salary

2. Why has he been able to keep this secret?

   a. He refuses to speak with the press.

   b. It's university policy.

   c. He's good at keeping secrets.

3. Why did he decide to reveal the secret now?

   a. The university told him he should reveal his salary.

   b. He had to because a reporter found out and made it public.

   c. He felt it was an important thing to do.

B. Complete the chart without looking at the text. Discuss your answers with a partner.

Information about Spanier	What the *Chronicle* found out
1. Spanier's salary	
2. Other types of compensation Spanier receives	
3. Total compensation compared to other university presidents	

5 | Understanding Apposition

REMEMBER

A word or phrase that means the same as a noun and is next to that noun in the sentence is said to be in apposition to the noun. See p. 89 for more information on *apposition*.

As you answer the following questions, think about why authors use apposition. Discuss your answers with a partner.

1. In the first paragraph, we find out through apposition what Graham B. Spanier does for a living. What does he do? _____

2. Underline the appositional phrase in the first paragraph.

3. Rewrite the first paragraph as three sentences instead of two, using *Spanier* or *he* as the subject of each sentence.

   _____

   _____

   _____

   _____

   _____

   _____

4. Why do you think the author uses apposition in the first paragraph?

   _____

   _____

   _____

6 | Understanding the Main Idea

Decide whether the first sentence of each paragraph in *Text 1* states the main idea. Check (✔) the correct answers and discuss them with a partner.

Paragraph	States the main idea	Does not state the main idea
¶1	☐	☐
¶2	☐	☐
¶3	☐	☐
¶4	☐	☐
¶5	☐	☐

7 | Detecting Sequence with Sequence Markers

Answer the following questions according to the text. Discuss your answers with a partner.

1. On what dates was Spanier's salary released? _____

   _____

2. Why was it released each time? _____

   _____

3. What are the sequence markers that helped you find this information?_____

   _____

8 | Understanding Subject Pronouns

Answer the following questions according to the text. Discuss your answers with a partner.

1. How many times does the name *Graham Spanier* appear?

   _____

2. How many subject pronouns refer to Graham Spanier? List them here.

   _____

   _____

3. How many times does the name *Stephen MacCarthy* appear?

   _____

4. How many subject pronouns refer to Stephen MacCarthy? List them here.

   _____

   _____

9 | Discussing the Issues

Answer the questions and discuss your answers with a partner.

1. Do you think Spanier's compensation package is too little, too much, or just right? Why?

2. Should public officials be required to make their salaries public?

3. Why do you think Spanier chose this time to make his salary public?

Text 2 | Keeping Illness Secret

1 | Getting Started

A. Answer the questions and briefly discuss your answers with a partner.

1. Do you know anyone who died after a serious illness?

2. If so, did you know that the person was ill?

3. If you did, did this help you to better handle the person's death?

B. Check (✔) whether you agree or disagree. Briefly discuss your answers with a partner.

Opinions about illness	Agree	Disagree
1. Doctors should tell patients if they have a serious illness.	☐	☐
2. Patients should discuss with their families if they have a serious illness.	☐	☐
3. Patients should share with their close friends if they have a serious illness.	☐	☐
4. Patients should inform a boss if they have a serious illness.	☐	☐

2 | Active Previewing

Preview the magazine article on the next page. Underline the title, the first sentence of each paragraph, and the last sentence of the text. Then answer the following questions with a partner.

The title of the article is "Should You Tell?" Should you tell what? In other words, what is the topic of the text?

3 | Reading and Recalling

A. Read the text. Stop after each paragraph and tell a partner two things you remember about it.

Should You Tell?

BY BETTY ROLLIN

1   Elaine Benson was the successful owner of an art gallery in the fashionable Hamptons in New York. Everyone knew her and most people liked her.

2   In 1995 she started feeling lousy. A visit to the doctor left her with a frightening diagnosis[1]: non-Hodgkin's lymphoma, a cancer of the lymphatic system[2]. It sounded serious, and she made one decision right away: with the exception of her husband and her daughter Kimberly, she would tell no one. Not anyone else in her family, not her close friends, not even her other children. She began chemotherapy[3], and her hair fell out. She got a wig that looked like a wig. A few of her friends asked her about it. In a weird coincidence[4], she was writing a book at the time about hair, so she told her friends that the wig was for research. They believed her.

3   Elaine gave Kimberly two reasons why she wanted to hide her disease: she thought it would undermine[5] the business, and she didn't want people feeling sorry for her. "I can't bear to have people look at me with sad eyes," she told her daughter.

4   Jimmie Holland, M.D., a psychiatrist in New York, sees many patients who have an impulse to hide. "They usually say they don't want pity[6]," says Holland. "But I don't know if that's what it really is. I think a lot of people feel a sense of shame about their illness, a loss of self-esteem."

> Your illness is your business. But keeping it a secret can cause damage of its own.

5   In the end, how to handle an illness is a very personal decision, though it can affect loved ones in a profound way. Elaine Benson's daughter (who lived nearby and saw so much of her mother that she had to be told) says other people were hurt by her mother's secrecy. "My brother and sister couldn't fathom that she didn't tell them. And there are friends who, for a long time, resented being shut out."

6   Despite this, Kimberly maintains that this was how her mother wanted to do it. She says that her mother's hiding her illness was the only way she felt she could continue being herself.

---

[1] **diagnosis:** the discovery of what a health problem is

[2] **lymphatic system:** part of the body's circulatory system

[3] **chemotherapy:** the use of drugs to control and/or try to cure cancer

[4] **coincidence:** when two seemingly unconnected things happen at the same time

[5] **undermine:** to gradually make something less strong

[6] **pity:** sympathy for someone who is suffering or unhappy

B. Read the text again without pausing. Tell your partner two new pieces of information that you remember.

C. Work as a class or in large groups. Say one thing you remember about the text.

4 | Understanding the Text

A. Complete as many statements as you can without looking at the text. Discuss your answers with a partner.

1. In 1995, Elaine Benson started to

    a. feel ill.

    b. worry about her daughters.

    c. sell paintings at a gallery.

2. She was diagnosed with a serious illness,

    a. diabetes.

    b. heart disease.

    c. non-Hodgkin's lymphoma, a cancer of the lymphatic system.

3. She began

    a. a long process to decide who to tell about her illness.

    b. chemotherapy, a cancer treatment.

    c. buying wigs for her research.

B. Check (✔) the correct answers according to the information in the text. Discuss your answers with a partner.

Elaine Benson ...	Yes	No
1. ... told Kimberly and her husband about her illness.	☐	☐
2. ... told her three children about her illness.	☐	☐
3. ... told her close friends about her illness.	☐	☐
4. ... refused chemotherapy.	☐	☐
5. ... went bald and wore a wig.	☐	☐

5 | Scanning

Practice scanning by doing the following. Discuss your answers with a partner.

1. A friend tells you a story about someone with cancer. You can't remember what the drug treatment is called that is mentioned in the article. Scan for the name.

2. Your teacher asks you to write a summary of the article but you can't remember the name of the woman the article is about. Scan for her name.

3. Your parents are visiting New York and you think they might like to visit the fashionable town where Ms. Benson has her gallery. Scan for the name of the town.

6 | Understanding Vocabulary in Context—Definitions

A. In the following sentence from the text, circle the words that are defined and underline the definition.

A visit to the doctor left her with a frightening diagnosis: non-Hodgkin's lymphoma, a cancer of the lymphatic system. (¶2)

B. Why does the author define this term and not others? Discuss your answer with a partner.

7 | Understanding Possessive Adjectives and Object Pronouns

A. Complete the chart according to the text. Then discuss your answers with a partner.

Possessive adjective	Who does it refer to?	How many times does it appear in the paragraph?
1. her (¶2)		
2. their (¶4)		
3. her (¶5)		

> **REMEMBER**
>
> A pronoun usually refers to the closest and/or most logical noun (or pronoun) that comes before it in a sentence or paragraph.
> See p. 43 for more information on *pronoun reference*.

B. Write the five sentences from the text that use *her* as an object pronoun.

1. _____

   _____

   _____

2. _____

   _____

   _____

3. _____

   _____

   _____

4. _____

   _____

   _____

5. _____

   _____

   _____

8 | Understanding Supporting Details

Write the opinion according to the two supporting details. Discuss your answers with a partner.

1. Elaine Benson's opinion: _____

Supporting details

    a She thought it would affect her business in a negative way.

    b. She didn't want people feeling sorry for her.

2. Jimmie Holland's opinion: _____

Supporting details

    a. "They usually say they don't want pity. "

    b. "But I don't know if that's what it really is. I think a lot of people feel a sense of shame about their illness, a loss of self-esteem."

3. Kimberly Benson's opinion: _____

Supporting details

    a. "My brother and sister couldn't fathom that she didn't tell them."

    b. "And there are friends who, for a long time, resented being shut out."

9 | Discussing the Issues

Answer the questions and discuss your answers with a partner.

1. Do you agree with Elaine Benson's decision?

2. If you were Kimberly Benson, or Elaine Benson's husband, would you have tried to convince Elaine to tell more people?

3. What, in your view, affects why a person might keep an illness secret: age, culture, gender, other things?

Text 3 | Secret Spenders

1 | Getting Started

Check (✔) the boxes that best describe your behaviors.

☐ 1. I sometimes hide purchases from my parents/spouse because he/she/they would lecture me.

☐ 2. I sometimes hide purchases from my parents/spouse because he/she/they would get angry.

☐ 3. I sometimes hide purchases from my parents/spouse because he/she/they would spend more as well.

☐ 4. I don't hide purchases.

Graphs and charts give a picture of statistical information. **Pie charts** show statistical information in the shape of a pie. Each "slice" of pie represents a part of the whole. A larger slice represents a larger percentage than the smaller slices. **Preview** graphs and charts by reading the title and any subtitles or category headings.

2 | Active Previewing

Preview the pie charts and answer the questions. Discuss your answers with a partner.

1. What is the main title of the charts? What information do you think will be provided?

2. What are the three subtitles? What information will be provided in each pie chart?

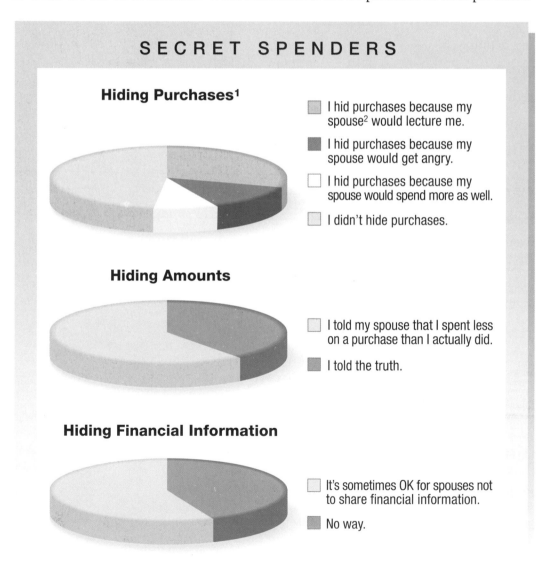

_____

[1] **purchases:** items bought

[2] **spouse:** husband or wife

3 | Scanning

Scan the pie charts for the answers. Discuss your answers with a partner.

1. In the chart titled *Hiding Purchases,* which group is the largest?

    a. the group who hid purchases because they were afraid to be yelled at

    b. the group who hid purchases because they didn't want to get a lecture

    c. the group who did not hide purchases

2. In the chart titled *Hiding Purchases,* which group is smaller?

    a. the group who hid the amount they spent

    b. the group who didn't hide amounts

    c. The groups are equal.

3. In the chart titled *Hiding Financial Information,* more people think it is

    a. never OK to keep financial information from a spouse.

    b. sometimes OK to keep financial information from a spouse.

    c. always OK to keep financial information from a spouse.

4. In the chart titled *Hiding Financial Information,* which group is smaller?

    a. the group who hid financial information

    b. the group who didn't hide financial information

    c. The groups are equal.

4 | Discussing the Issues

Answer the questions and discuss your answers with a partner.

1. According to the pie charts, do more people think keeping spending secret is OK or not OK?

2. How do you explain this fact?

3. In your opinion, is it accurate? Do more people share information rather than hide it?

Text 4 | Lie Detection

1 | Getting Started

A. Answer the questions and briefly discuss your answers with a partner.

1. Have you ever been lied to? How do you know?

2. Have you ever lied? If so, was the lie successful?

B. Check (✔) the statements that reflect your opinion. Briefly discuss your answers with a partner.

☐ 1. It is quite easy to figure out if someone is lying.

☐ 2. It is quite difficult to tell if someone is lying.

☐ 3. Trained professionals like police officers have an easier time telling if a person is lying.

☐ 4. A person who is lying will look away from the person he's lying to.

☐ 5. A person who is lying will shift his/her body more.

☐ 6. A person who is lying blinks less than someone who is not lying.

☐ 7. A person who is lying changes his story often.

☐ 8. A person who is lying sticks with one story, but it doesn't have a lot of detail.

2 | Active Previewing

Preview the academic text on the next page. Underline the title, the first sentence of each paragraph, and the last sentence of the text. Then answer the following questions with a partner.

1. What is the text about?

2. In what class might a student expect to read this text?

3 | Reading and Recalling

A. Read the text. Stop after each paragraph and tell a partner two things that you remember about it.

Deception Detection

Psychologists Try to Learn How to Spot a Liar

by Carrie Lock

1 "Is he lying?" You'll probably never know. Although people have been communicating with one another for tens of thousands of years, more than 30 years of psychological research has found that most people are very poor lie detectors[1].

2 In the only worldwide study of its kind, scientists asked more than 2,000 people from nearly 60 countries a question. "How can you tell when people are lying?" From Botswana to Belgium, the number-one answer was the same: Liars look away from the person they're lying to. "This is... the most prevalent stereotype[2] about deception in the world," says Charles Bond of Texas Christian University in Fort Worth. Mr. Bond led the research project. And yet looking away, like other commonly held stereotypes about liars, isn't connected with lying at all, studies have shown. Liars don't shift around or touch their noses or clear their throats any more than truth tellers do.

3 For decades, psychologists have done laboratory experiments in an attempt to describe differences between the behavior of liars and people telling the truth. One thing is certain: There is no unique obvious signal for a fib.

Common Behaviors

4 By studying large groups of participants, researchers have identified certain general behaviors that liars are more likely to have than people who are telling the truth. Fibbers tend to move their arms, hands, and fingers less and blink less than people telling the truth do. Liars' voices can become more tense or high. Liars may move less and fill their speech with pauses because they are trying too hard to remember what they've already said and to keep their stories consistent. People shading the truth tend to make fewer speech errors than truth tellers do. They rarely backtrack to fill in forgotten or incorrect details. "Their stories are too good to be true," says Bella dePaulo of the University of California, Santa Barbara, who has written several reviews of the field of deception research.

5 Liars may also feel fear and guilt or excitement at fooling people. Such emotions can

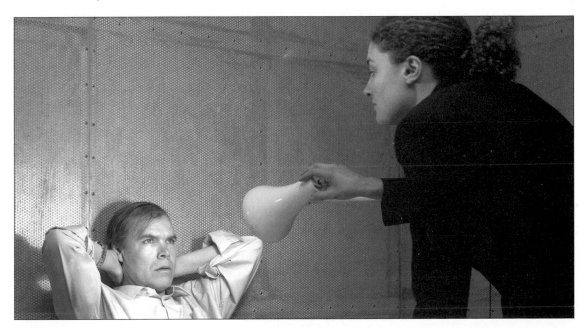

continued

---

[1] **lie detectors:** machines, or in this case people, who can tell if someone is lying

[2] **stereotype:** a fixed idea of what a particular type of person or thing is like

continued

trigger a change in facial expression so short that most observers never notice. Paul Ekman, a retired psychologist from the University of California, San Francisco, calls these split-second changes "micro expressions." He says these emotional clues, such as a smile, a grimace[3] , or a wince[4], are as important as gestures, voice, and speech patterns in uncovering deceitfulness.

6   But not all liars show these signals. One can't conclude people are lying because they don't move their arms or pause while telling stories. These could be natural behaviors for them, not signs of lying. "They are statistically reliable indicators[5]

of deception," says Timothy Levine of Michigan State University in East Lansing. But that doesn't mean they're helpful in one-on-one encounters.

7   People are just not very good at spotting deception signals. On average, over hundreds of laboratory studies, participants distinguish correctly between truths and lies only about 55 percent of the time. This success rate holds for groups as diverse as students and police officers. "Human accuracy is really just barely better than chance," says dePaulo.

---

[3] **grimace:** a facial expression showing pain, disgust, or contempt

[4] **wince:** a small sudden movement expressing unpleasantness

[5] **indicators:** signs or pieces of evidence

B. Read the text again without pausing. Tell your partner two new pieces of information that you remember.

C. Work as a class or in large groups. Say one thing you remember about the text.

4 | Understanding the Text

A. Answer as many questions as you can without looking at the text. Discuss your answers with a partner.

1. What has 30 years of psychological research shown about lie detection?

   a. People are really good at detecting a liar.

   b. Police officers and other trained professionals are really good at detecting a liar.

   c. People are not very good at detecting a liar.

2. One stereotype about liars held by people all around the world is that

   a. a liar speaks very slowly and clearly.

   b. a liar looks away.

   c. a liar gets confused and changes stories.

3. Scientists came to the conclusion that people are not good at detecting liars because studies show that people can tell the difference between truth and lies only

  a. 5% of the time.

  b. 55% of the time.

  c. 90% of the time.

B. Check (✔) behaviors that liars are more likely to exhibit, according to the text. Discuss your answers with a partner.

  ☐ **1.** Liars move less.

  ☐ **2.** Liars' voices become tense or high.

  ☐ **3.** Liars look away.

  ☐ **4.** Liars blink less.

  ☐ **5.** Liars make fewer speech errors.

  ☐ **6.** Liars tell confusing stories, correcting themselves a lot.

  ☐ **7.** Liars fill their speech with pauses.

  ☐ **8.** Liars touch their noses.

5 | Understanding Vocabulary in Context—Synonyms

Complete the chart below with synonyms used in the text for *lying/lie* **(noun),** *liar* **(noun), and** *lying/lie* **(verb). Briefly discuss your answers with a partner.**

Lying/Lie (noun)	Liar (noun)	Lying/Lie (verb)
¶2	¶4	¶4
¶3		
¶5		

6 | Understanding Topic, Main Idea, and Supporting Details

A. Text. Answer the following questions and briefly discuss your answers with a partner.

1. What is the topic of the text? _____

2. What is the main idea of the text? _____

B. Paragraphs. Answer the following questions. Discuss your answers with a partner.

1. What is the main idea of ¶2?

   _____

2. What are two supporting details for ¶2?

   _____

   _____

   _____

3. What is the main idea of ¶4?

   _____

   _____

4. What are two supporting details for ¶4?

   _____

   _____

   _____

7 | Understanding Vocabulary in Context—Examples

Reread ¶5. Then answer the following questions and discuss your answers with a partner.

1. What is the concept?

   _____

2. What are the examples?

   _____

3. What words are used to signal the examples?

   _____

8 | Discussing the Issues

Answer the questions and discuss your answers with a partner.

1. Were you surprised by what you learned from the text? Why or why not?

2. Why do you think it's so hard to tell if someone is lying?

3. Do you think it's possible that people could be trained to be better lie detectors?

Putting It On Paper

A. Write a paragraph on one of these topics.

1. Should children be taught not to lie? Why or why not?

2. Do people who keep illnesses secret deserve our understanding?

3. Should police officers or psychologists be better trained in detecting liars?

Steps for your paragraph

a. State your opinion in the first sentence; this is your topic sentence.

b. Write three sentences with details—facts, data, examples, etc.—that prove your opinion.

c. Summarize your ideas in a final sentence.

B. Exchange paragraphs with a partner. Read your partner's paragraph and answer the questions in the checklist. Give feedback to your partner.

✔ CHECKLIST
1. Can you identify your partner's opinion about the topic?
2. Are there three examples to support the topic? Number them on the paper.
3. Are you persuaded by your partner's examples or reasons? Explain below.
4. Is any of the information not related to the topic? If yes, please underline it on your partner's paper and then write it below.

_____

_____

_____

_____

_____

_____

_____

C. Revise your work based on your partner's feedback.

Taking It Online | Keeping Secrets

A. With a partner, use the Internet to research keeping salaries or money secret, keeping illness secret, or lie detection.

1. Together, decide which topic you would like to know more about. Make a list of four questions you still have about the topic.

   _____

   _____

   _____

   _____

2. Use Google (www.google.com) or another major search engine to begin your online research.

3. Preview the sites as you would a magazine article or an essay.

B. Complete the table with the information you find.

> **ONLINE TIP**
>
> If you use the word "secret" or "secrets" in your search, you will come up with a lot of sites offering tips for how to do something. You will need to ignore many of those and look for the sites that use the word in the way you mean it.

Your topic:
Information similar to information in this chapter:
Information different from information in this chapter:
Your conclusions:

C. Following up. Share with your classmates the most interesting things you learned about secrets.

Vocabulary Index

S

T

W

Skills and Strategies Index

Reading Skills

Detecting Sequence with Sequence Markers, 123, 124, 128, 136, 144

Previewing

Bar Graphs, 45, 129
Charts, 108
Line Graphs, 69
Maps, 9
Newspaper Articles, **19**, 37, 73, 80, 104, 140
Online Articles, Magazine Articles, and Academic
   Texts, **3**, 7, 12, 24, 30, 41, 48, 58, 63, 86, 93, 100,
   111, 120, 125, 132, 145, 152
Pictographs, **27**
Pie Charts, **150**
Timelines, **90**

Scanning

Graphics, **10**, 11, 47, 70, 108, 131, 151
Pictographs, **28**, 29
Texts, **37**, 49, 58, 63, 73, 93, 125, 147

Skimming, 132

Understanding

Bar Graphs, **45**, 129
Charts, **108**
Line Graphs, **69**
Main Idea, **84**, 85, 89, 96, 143, 156
Maps, **9**
Pictographs, **27**
Pie Charts, **150**
Supporting Details, **103**, 104, 107, 116, 135, 149,
   156
Timelines, **90**
Topic, **61**, 62, 66, 67, 75, 76, 89, 156

Vocabulary Strategies

Skipping Words, **2**, 3, 6, 7, 12, 19, 24, 30, 36, 40

Understanding

Possessive Adjectives, **106**, 107, 123, 148
Subject and Object Pronouns, **43**, 44, 52, 76, 83,
   144, 148
Vocabulary in Context
   Apposition, **89**, 115, 143
   Definitions, **22**, 23, 26, 32, 53, 54, 62, 67, 115,
   116, 148
   Examples, **124**, 128, 156
   Synonyms, **53**, 54, 71, 72, 155

Photo Credits

Jupiter Images, George Hall p. 1 (ferry); Alamy, Peter Bowater **p. 1** (French TGV train); Jupiter Images, p. 1 (covered wagon); Map Resources, **p. 5** (map of the world); Jupiter Images, David Scott Smith **p. 7** (RV); Underwood Photo Archives/SuperStock, Thomas Winz **p. 13** (railroad workers in the 1930's); Getty Images, Roger Ressmeyer & Gerry Ellis-Globio **p. 17** (Indian tiger); Oxford Scientific /Jupiter Images, Stan Osolinski p. 17 (white rhino); Nature PL, Luiz Claudio Marigo **p. 17** (sea turtle); Eagle Visions Photography, Craig Lowell **p. 17** (panda); Earth Scenes/Animals Animals, Keren Su **p. 18** (pandas habitat); ChinaChengduPanda, **p. 20** (two pandas); Photo Researchers. Jphn Shaw **p. 21** (toy koala); China Photos/Getty Images, **p. 21** (panda released); Brand X Pictures/Jupiter Images, Rob Casey **p. 21** (bamboo); Earth Scenes/Animals Animals, Joe McDonald **p. 23** (tiger's habitat); Getty Images, Mark Wilson p. 25 (Indian tigers); Mary Evans PL, **p. 29** (wooly mammoth); Peter Arnold, Inc./Alamy, **p. 29** (ivory-billed woodpecker); Bruce Coleman, Raymond Tercafs **p. 29** (coelacanth); Bristol City Museum/Nature PL, **p. 29** (dodo);); Bruce Coleman, Jen & Jen & Des Bartlett **p. 29** (servaline genet); Banana Stock/Jupiter Images, p. 35 (pumpkin seeds); Banana Stock/Jupiter Images, **p. 35** (flower bulbs); Photo Edit Inc., Robert W. Gin **p. 35** (peanuts); Mediacolor's/Alamy, **p. 36** (pumpkin patch); Diana Dill-MacDonald, **p. 38** (Howard Dill and his giant pumpkin); Reuters, Mike Hutchings **p. 40** (Nelson Mandela); Reuters, Rick Wilking **p. 41** (Nelson Mandela); Nature PL, Jose B. Ruiz **p. 48** (orchid); Bruce Coleman, Mark Taylor **p. 49** (orchid); Photographers Direct, Buddy Mays **p. 50** (Costa Rica rainforest); Aflo Foto Agency/Age FotoStock, **p. 57** (swimmer); Reuters, Dylan Martinez **p. 57** (runner); Photo Edit Inc., Davis Barber **p. 57** (bicyclist); Aurora, Corey Rich **p. 58** (yoga); Reuters, Alex Grimm **p. 59** (ironman competition); Corbis, **p. 65** (Lynne Cox in 1987); Reuters, Andy Mueller **p. 65** (Tegla Loroupe); Bettman/Corbis, **p. 65** (Chuhei Nambu); Bongarts/Getty Images, Alexander Hassenstein **p. 65** (Katerina Neumannova);

Polaris, Paul Martinka **p. 68** (NYC Marathon); Photo Edit Inc., Jonathan Nourok **p. 74** (Special Olympics); Getty Images, Donald Uhrbrock **p. 79** (moveable type); Fancy Photography/Veer, **p. 79** (new Mac); Bildarchiv Preussischer Kulturbesitz/Art Resource, NY, **p. 79** (messenger); Photo Edit Inc., Nancy Sheehan **p. 80** (toddlers in a sandbox);); Photo Edit Inc., Christina Kennedy **p. 81** (baby sign language); Age FotoStock, Martin Siepmann **p. 87** (La Gomera Island); Punchstock, **p. 94** (teen on computer); Creatas/Age FotoStock, **p. 99** (healer); Blend Images/Punchstock, Tanya Constantine **p. 99** (health food store); Age FotoStock, Peter Holmes **p. 99** (herbs); Prisma/SuperStock, **p. 101** (Chinese herbs); Photo Edit Inc., Mary Kate Denny **p. 105** (sneezing); Getty Images, Garry Gay **p. 108** (sweets); Masterfile, **p. 110** (tea ceremony in Japan); Image Source/Age Fotostock, **p. 110** (teens drinking soda); Danita Delimont, Kalpana Kartik **p. 111** (cafe in the Middle East); Masterfile, Andrew Olney **p. 111** (coffee shop); Corbis/Jupiter Images, **p. 112** (drinking coffee); Alamy, Cristian Baitg Schreiweis **p. 113** (coffee and coffee beans); Jupiter Images, Cornelia Doerr **p. 119** (gorilla); Jupiter Images, Manfred Pfefferle **p. 119** (lady slipper orchid); Getty Images, Tom Boyle **p. 119** (cell on a slide); Index Stock, Frank Staub **p. 121** (bridge in rainforest); The Image Works, **p. 126** (Alexander Flemming); Avatra Images/Alamy, **p. 129** (sleeping); Scanpix/Reuters, **p. 133** (Dr. Warren and Dr. Marshall); Photo Edit Inc., David Young-Wolff **p. 139** (telling a secret); Getty Images, Chip Somodevill **p. 139** (White House Press Secretary); Photo Edit Inc., Rahcel Epstein **p. 139** (two adults talking); Photo Edito Inc., David Young Wolff **p. 140** (money); Alamy, Andre Jenny **p. 141** (State College U of P); Jerzyworks/Masterfile, **p. 146** (Dr. & patient); The Image Bank/Getty Images, Alan Thornton **p. 153** (police interrogation).

Art Credits

Barb Bastian: **p. 28**, **91**; Arlene Boehm: **p. 46**; Annie Bissett: **p. 70**, **150**; Karen Minot: **p. 10**, **130**.